## W9-CYF-851

*Gift of the*
*Hackbarth Foundation*
*2015*

# Premenstrual Disorders

# THE STATE OF MENTAL ILLNESS AND ITS THERAPY

# THE STATE OF MENTAL ILLNESS AND ITS THERAPY

## Premenstrual Disorders

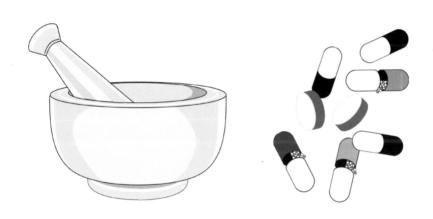

### Sherry Bonnice

Mason Crest

Mason Crest
450 Parkway Drive, Suite D
Broomall, PA 19008
www.masoncrest.com

Printed in the Hashemite Kingdom of Jordan.

First printing
9 8 7 6 5 4 3 2 1

Series ISBN: 978-1-4222-2819-7
ISBN: 978-1-4222-2833-3
ebook ISBN: 978-1-4222-8994-5

The Library of Congress has cataloged the
      hardcopy format(s) as follows:

      Library of Congress Cataloging-in-Publication Data

Bonnice, Sherry, 1956-
    [Drug therapy and premenstrual disorders]
    Premenstrual disorders / Sherry Bonnice.
      pages cm. – (The state of mental illness and its therapy)
    Audience: Age 12.
    Audience: Grade 7 to 8.
    Revision of: Drug therapy and premenstrual disorders. 2004.
    Includes bibliographical references and index.
    ISBN 978-1-4222-2833-3 (hardcover) – ISBN 978-1-4222-2819-7 (series) – ISBN 978-1-4222-8994-5 (ebook)
    1. Premenstrual syndrome–Juvenile literature. 2. Premenstrual syndrome–Chemotherapy–Juvenile literature. 3. Premenstrual syndrome–Alternative treatment–Juvenile literature. I. Title.
    RG165.B66 2014
    618.1'72061–dc23
                        2013008232

Produced by Vestal Creative Services.

www.vestalcreative.com

This book is meant to educate and should not be used as an alternative to appropriate medical care. Its creators have made every effort to ensure that the information presented is accurate—but it is not intended to substitute for the help and services of trained professionals.

Picture Credits:
Andreus | Dreamstime.com: p. 50. Ariwasabi | Dreamstime.com: p. 12. Artville: p. 102, 105. Autumn Libal: pp. 19, 20, 40. Benjamin Stewart: p. 39. Chuyu | Dreamstime.com: p. 93, 94. Corbis: pp. 110, 121, 122. Corel: pp. 35, 104. Edmandarina | Dreamstime.com: p. 14. Dreamstime.com Agency | Dreamstime.com: p. 111. Feng Yu | Dreamstime.com: p. 65. Feverpitched | Dreamstime.com: p. 25. Franant | Dreamstime.com: p. 22. Galina Barskaya | Dreamstime.com: p. 70. Helder Almeida | Dreamstime.com: p. 26. Hilary Rivers | Dreamstime.com: p. 90. Image Source: pp. 54, 60, 66, 106. Ioana Grecu | Dreamstime.com: p. 46. Iurii Davydov | Dreamstime.com: p. 56. Jason Stitt | Dreamstime.com: pp. 23, 74, 88. Kelliem | Dreamstime.com: p. 100. Marcelo Poleze | Dreamstime.com: p. 30. Martinmark | Dreamstime.com: p. 114. National Library of Medicine: p. 78. Nyul | Dreamstime.com: p. 80. Paul Hakimata | Dreamstime.com: p. 49. PhotoDisc: pp. 32, 36, 58, 63, 69, 72, 85, 86, 96, 97, 98, 108, 113, 114. Photoeuphoria | Dreamstime.com: p. 84. Photo Alto: p. 10. Rubberball: pp. 53, 83, 107. Steven Cukrov | Dreamstime.com: p. 118. Stockbyte: p. 88. The individuals in these images are models, and the images are for illustrative purposes only. To the best knowledge of the publisher, all other images are in the public domain. If any image has been inadvertently uncredited or miscredited, please notify Vestal Creative Services, Vestal, New York 13850, so that rectification can be made for future printings.

# CONTENTS

# Introduction
## by Mary Ann McDonnell

Teenagers have reason to be interested in psychiatric disorders and their treatment. Friends, family members, and even teens themselves may experience one of these disorders. Using scenarios adolescents will understand, this series explains various psychiatric disorders and the drugs that treat them.

Diagnosis and treatment of psychiatric disorders in children between six and eighteen years old are well studied and documented in the scientific journals. A paper appearing in the *Journal of the American Academy of Child and Adolescent Psychiatry* in 2010 estimated that 49.5 percent of all adolescents aged 13 to 18 were affected by at least one psychiatric disorder. Various other studies have reported similar findings. Needless to say, many children and adolescents are suffering from psychiatric disorders and are in need of treatment.

Many children have more than one psychiatric disorder, which complicates their diagnoses and treatment plans. Psychiatric disorders often occur together. For instance, a person with a sleep disorder may also be depressed; a teenager with attention-deficit/hyperactivity disorder (ADHD) may also have a substance-use disorder. In psychiatry, we call this comorbidity. Much research addressing this issue has led to improved diagnosis and treatment.

The most common child and adolescent psychiatric disorders are anxiety disorders, depressive disorders, and ADHD. Sleep disorders, sexual disorders, eating disorders, substance-abuse disorders, and psychotic disorders are also quite common. This series has volumes that address each of these disorders.

Major depressive disorders have been the most commonly diagnosed mood disorders for children and adolescents. Researchers don't agree as to how common mania and bipolar disorder are in children. Some experts believe that manic episodes in children and adolescents are underdiagnosed. Many times, a mood disturbance may occur with another psychiatric disorder. For instance, children with ADHD may also be depressed. ADHD is just one psychiatric disorder that is a major health concern for children, adolescents, and adults. Studies of ADHD have reported prevalence rates among children that range from two to 12 percent.

Failure to understand or seek treatment for psychiatric disorders puts children and young adults at risk of developing substance-use disorders. For example, recent research indicates that those with ADHD who were treated with medication were 85 percent less likely to develop a substance-use disorder. Results like these emphasize the importance of timely diagnosis and treatment.

Early diagnosis and treatment may prevent these children from developing further psychological problems. Books like those in this series provide important information, a vital first step toward increased awareness of psychological disorders; knowledge and understanding can shed light on even the most difficult subject. These books should never, however, be viewed as a substitute for professional consultation. Psychiatric testing and an evaluation by a licensed professional is recommended to determine the needs of the child or adolescent and to establish an appropriate treatment plan.

# Foreword
## by Donald Esherick

We live in a society filled with technology—from computers surfing the Internet to automobiles operating on gas and batteries. In the midst of this advanced society, diseases, illnesses, and medical conditions are treated and often cured with the administration of drugs, many of which were unknown thirty years ago. In the United States, we are fortunate to have an agency, the Food and Drug Administration (FDA), which monitors the development of new drugs and then determines whether the new drugs are safe and effective for use in human beings.

When a new drug is developed, a pharmaceutical company usually intends that drug to treat a single disease or family of diseases. The FDA reviews the company's research to determine if the drug is safe for use in the population at large and if it effectively treats the targeted illnesses. When the FDA finds that the drug is safe and effective, it approves the drug for treating that specific disease or condition. This is called the labeled indication.

During the routine use of the drug, the pharmaceutical company and physicians often observe that a drug treats other medical conditions besides what is indicated in the labeling. While the labeling will not include the treatment of the particular condition, a physician can still prescribe the drug to a patient with this disease. This is known as an unlabeled or off-label indication. This series contains information about both the labeled and off-label indications of psychiatric drugs.

I have reviewed the books in this series from the perspective of the pharmaceutical industry and the FDA, specifically focusing on the labeled indications, uses, and known side effects of these drugs. Further information can be found on the FDA's website (www.FDA.gov).

When a girl is experiencing PMS symptoms, she may find it more difficult to interact with others.

# Chapter One

# Defining Premenstrual Syndrome

Emily Palmer's Journal, September 12

*I can't believe Sarah has to be so difficult. She always has to have her own way and then when we disagree, she blames it on me. She has some nerve, telling me I'm a baby for missing school when I have my period. Me, Emily Palmer, a baby? She knows I'm not! Yesterday she and Laura were making faces when I cried after we got our reports back. I worked hard on that assignment, and she knows it better than anyone else. Why can't she understand? She's supposed to be my best friend. And today she went and brought up my sweat-*

pants and my zits in the same sentence. When my face breaks out, I could die. And I can't help it if my jeans were tight and I had to change. We were only hanging around the house anyway. Does she think I have to be a fashion statement every minute? Mom probably shrunk my jeans anyway, my favorite pair of jeans. She says she didn't put them in the dryer, but what else could it be? I don't think I've pigged out lately; well, just those chips Sarah and I ate Friday night, and let's see, those chocolate donuts, but anyway, I didn't eat so much my jeans shouldn't fit. Well, at least Sarah and I had fun that night! We watched our favorite chick flick. Sarah imitated one of the actors. She is so funny. Why does she have to bother me when most of the time she's fun? Maybe I shouldn't have yelled at her and told her to go home today, but what else could I do? I could hardly control myself I was so angry. If I hadn't sent her home, I just don't

During the week before menstruating, a woman's appetite may increase.

*know what I would have done or said. I didn't mean it. Mom heard the whole thing, though, and now she thinks I'm out of control. She wants me to see a doctor. Just because I'm a little grouchy before I get my period! I hate my period—and I hate going to the doctor!!!*

Like Emily, some teenage girls resent their monthly cycle. Most girls, though, consider their first menstruation an important time in their life. Years later, they can tell how old they were that day and where they were when it happened; some even remember what they were wearing. Many cultures consider a young girl's first menstruation to be a cause for celebration; she is then considered mature and able to have her own family. This wonderful event marks the beginning of the female's reproductive years.

But Emily isn't the only young woman to feel as though she hates her menstrual cycle. Many individuals and groups have spent years trying to correct the false ideas promoted throughout history. A woman who is menstruating is not "unclean." She is not sick, nor is she imagining her symptoms. Menstruation is a natural part of life with many real and wonderful aspects.

Unfortunately, premenstrual syndrome is also a reality. Today, many doctors recognize the significance of a woman's menstrual cycle and the way it affects her. With the help of research and good medical care this recognition has led to a positive understanding of ways a woman can deal with her monthly changes.

A girl's first menstrual period usually occurs sometime between the age of ten and sixteen. The first time ovulation occurs is not until about two years after the first period, and it may not occur regularly each month for a while after that. But even though young girls' periods are not regular and they are not even ovulating yet, they may, like Emily, experience emotional and physical changes they do not understand. Some of these feelings may be difficult to handle.

ovulation: The release of a mature egg (ovum) from the ovary.

**herpes:** A group of inflammatory viral diseases of the skin. Includes cold sores and sexually transmitted diseases.

**heart palpitations:** Rapid or irregular beating of the heart.

**puberty:** The beginning of the period in which someone is able to reproduce sexually.

A girl who is experiencing PMS may feel depressed or irritable.

Some of the major symptoms of premenstrual syndrome (PMS) include a depressed mood, headaches, anxiety, emotional instability, a bloated feeling, and a decrease of interest in usual activities. As many as 150 symptoms associated with the syndrome may disrupt normal daily functioning.

The symptoms are sometimes easier to understand if they are divided into two categories: the physical and the emotional (behavioral). Some physical symptoms include backaches, abdominal bloating and pain, tightness of rings and shoes, breast tenderness, acne, skin rashes, outbreaks of herpes, sinus congestion, increased vaginal secretions, worsening of asthma symptoms, muscle spasms and pain in arms and legs (especially the joints), dizziness, tiredness, lack of coordination, heart palpitations, changes in appetite, di-

Which of the following statements are true of your monthly menstrual cycle?

- I miss school or athletic practice because I am too ill to participate.
- I cry frequently.
- I feel depressed and not myself.
- I'm so angry I find myself arguing over almost nothing.
- Many times I feel I am insignificant.
- I feel very sad.
- I don't feel like going out with any of my friends or doing the things I normally enjoy.
- I can't sit still. I find myself pacing and unable to concentrate.
- I think the same thoughts over and over again.
- I feel out of control.
- I'm so tired.
- I can't help eating chocolate, potato chips, or other sugary or high-fat food.
- I can't seem to sleep even though I am exhausted.
- My clothes get too tight.
- I have headaches.
- My breasts are sore.
- If you have checked true to several of these statements you should check with your physician about PMS.

Information based on the American Psychiatric Association's *Diagnostic and Statistical Manual of Mental Disorders*.

**menopause:** The time of the natural cessation of menstruation, usually after age 45.

**menses:** The menstrual flow.

arrhea or constipation, insomnia, and weight gain. Behavioral symptoms, which can cause mild to severe personality changes, include tension, irritability, depression, anxiety, mood swings, outbreaks of temper, forgetfulness, aggression, indecisiveness, and difficulty concentrating.

Symptoms may begin at any time during a woman's childbearing years, from puberty through menopause. They usually disappear while pregnant and after menopause. Symptoms may differ from month to month, or they may remain the same. One woman may have only one symptom, or she may suffer from a variety of physical and emotional symptoms. The severity also varies, some months being milder, followed by more distressful menses.

Like Emily, Martie could not understand why she was having trouble in school at certain times and not others. For most of the month, Martie got As and Bs, played on the softball team, and worked part time at a local floral shop. She loved it all. But she had been noticing that sometimes she just didn't want to go to practice, and she found herself making excuses for not being able to work.

Once she told her boss she was so tired she had to go home to bed. And she did go home and took a nap. But later that day she started her period. She felt so much better she went out with her friends to a movie; to her embarrassment, she ran into her boss outside the theater. She hadn't lied about being so tired and she did feel better later in the day—but she knew her boss thought she had wanted to skip work so she could have a good time with her friends. Martie felt guilty. She didn't know what was wrong with her.

Symptoms like these are difficult to understand. If women do not comprehend the link between their feelings and their menstrual cycle, these symptoms may cause problems in their personal and work relationships.

# A Woman's Cycle

Menstruation is considered the beginning of a woman's cycle. Whether it begins at the end, the middle, or the beginning of the calendar month, the first five or more days while a woman menstruates mark the start of her menstrual cycle. Any premenstrual symptoms she might have experienced in the previous week should disappear during this time and stay away throughout the follicular phase, which lasts until about the fourteenth day after the start of her period. During this phase, the follicle cells of the ovary begin increasing in size. They also produce the hormone estrogen, which causes the lining of the uterus to begin thickening in preparation for an egg to be fertilized.

follicle cells: Vesicles in the ovary that contain the egg surrounded by a covering of cells.

hormone: A product of living cells that circulates in the body and produces a specific effect on cells.

On day fourteen or fifteen, an egg is released by the graafian follicle, the largest follicle, when estrogen levels are at their highest. During the next twelve to thirty-six hours, the egg can be fertilized if the woman has sexual intercourse. Throughout the luteal phase, high levels of estrogen and progesterone exist for the nourishment of the egg in case it should be fertilized. Many women experiences symptoms during this one- to two-week time before menstruation begins. If fertilization does not happen, hormone levels begin to decrease, and the lining of the uterus thins out as menstruation starts. Some women experience premenstrual symptoms during this time as well.

Everyone feels upset sometimes; everyone gets depressed once in a while; and we all experience changes in our appetite and energy level. But when the pattern is clear and consistent over various months, this helps to confirm an association between these symptoms and the menstrual cycle.

Because of the cyclical nature of these symptoms, physicians and researchers study calendar charts of women who suspect they suffer from PMS. These records chart various symptoms for three menstrual cycles. By recording when a symptom appears each month, the severity of it, and the duration, the physician and patient are able to determine if PMS is the problem or if there is another disease causing the condition.

Charts differ in the way they are laid out, but they all serve the same purpose. By charting symptoms, a permanent record exists that allows the sufferer and the physician to diagnose and treat PMS. Symptoms will appear on the chart in clusters rather than random distribution throughout the month. One of the benefits of charting is that women realize their symptoms only last for a certain number of days. Knowing that headaches, backache, and bloating will end within a week may make the pain easier to endure.

PMS can only occur from the time of ovulation until menstruation begins. At this time, the production of progesterone is increased. Besides progesterone's effect on the uterus, the increase in progesterone is now being studied for its effect on certain chemicals in the brain. It may be that the accelerated hormone levels cause a decrease in the availability or action of the brain chemicals, specifically the neurotransmitter serotonin. But this is still only one of the ideas as to why monthly changes exist in a woman's mind and body. There are no specific tests to prove this theory or any others. That is why the use of a chart is so critical. With no other medical tests to verify the presence of PMS, it is important to have this written record of when the symptoms occur each month.

According to the obstetricians and gynecologists treating this condition, about 20 to 40 percent of all women have PMS symptoms. (Of course, these numbers may be low because many women who have these symptoms assume they are simply an ordinary part of life and never mention them to their

obstetricians: Physicians who specialize in pregnancy and birth.

gynecologists: Physicians who specialize in the reproductive systems of women.

# Diagnosing PMS and PMDD in Adolescents

Because there is no exact testing for PMS or PMDD, confirming a diagnosis takes time and effort on the part of the patient. Teenage girls are especially prone to blame mood swings and temper on the ups and downs that occur in their relationships, on their demanding schedules, and on their desire to be set apart from the adults in their lives.

For this reason, it is important that young women take responsibility for their own health by charting and logging in a diary how they feel each month. Some women feel they are going crazy, that they aren't like everyone else, and that no one understands. Find someone who does understand—a friend, an aunt, or a teacher. Getting the right kind of help can make a difference for the rest of your life.

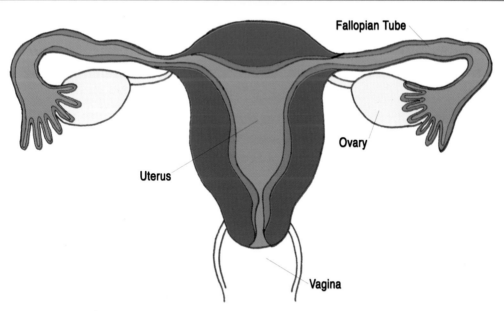

A woman's reproductive system releases powerful hormones; these chemicals will fluctuate, depending on where she is in her monthly cycle.

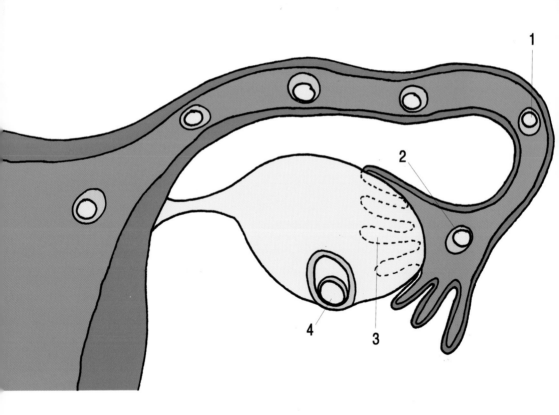

During a woman's menstrual cycle, she may experience emotional ups and downs, which are caused by the changes taking place inside her body. Numbers 1 through 4 show the egg at various stages in its progress from the ovary, down through the Fallopian tube (3), into the uterus. When the egg is first released from the ovary (4), estrogen levels are at their highest. Estrogen and progesterone (the two main female hormones) remain high through the next couple of weeks, during the time when the egg is ready to be fertilized (2,1). The woman can become pregnant during this time, but she does not usually experience PMS symptoms until the hormone levels begin to drop. As the hormone levels fall, her uterus's lining begins to thin, and menstruation takes place—and the woman's emotional level may take a dip as well.

physicians.) Another five to six percent are affected so much by their PMS symptoms that their daily lives are severely disrupted during this time. These women suffer from premenstrual dysphoric disorder (PMDD), a less prevalent but more distressful form of PMS recognized by the American Psychiatric Association (APA) as a "depressive disorder." Although PMDD shares the same symptoms as PMS, it differs in the severity of the symptoms and the necessity of specific treatment to control them.

# Premenstrual Dysphoric Disorder

According to the fourth edition of the American Psychiatric Association's *Diagnostic and Statistical Manual of Mental Disorders, Fourth Edition, Text Revision* (DSM-IV-TR), a diagnosis of PMDD can be made when five or more of the following symptoms are consistently present during the first week of the luteal phase, with at least one symptom being among the first four listings:

1.  feeling sad, hopeless, or down on yourself
2.  feeling tense, anxious or "on edge"
3.  marked instability of mood interspersed with frequent tearfulness
4.  persistent irritability, anger, and increased interpersonal conflicts
5.  decreased interest in usual activities, which may be associated with withdrawal from social relationships
6.  difficulty concentrating
7.  feeling fatigued, lethargic, or lacking in energy
8.  marked changes in appetite, including binge eating or food cravings
9.  hypersomnia (excessive sleeping) or insomnia (lack of sleep)
10. feeling overwhelmed or out of control
11. physical symptoms such as breast tenderness, headaches, bloating, weight gain, or muscle or joint pain

When a physician treats a woman with PMS or PMDD, she may try various treatment methods, including diet changes, exercise, diurectics, and hormone therapy, as well as psychiatric drugs. If a woman continues to experience symptoms, the physician may feel the patient needs a psychiatric evaluation. A physician who works closely with a psychologist or a psychiatrist may more quickly make an accurate evaluation. Even if the physician does conclude that the patient has PMDD, a therapist might uncover some issues that could prove helpful when trying to gain a more complete recovery. For instance, Emily might find that she tries too hard to please people. As she makes decisions based on what she knows is right rather than what she thinks will make Sarah or any of her other friends most happy, she will feel better about herself and more in control of her life. Feelings like these add to general well-being, no matter what the patient is dealing with medically.

Many women experience PMS symptoms, but only a few will suffer from PMDD.

Premenstrual disorders may make it hard for friends to get along.

epilepsy: Any of various disorders characterized by a disturbance of the electrical rhythm of the central nervous system, frequently manifested by convulsions.

If a woman has PMDD, these symptoms will be so severe that they interfere with work, school, usual social activities, and her relationships with others. Many times grade scores are lower at this time; a woman who normally completes her work easily will have trouble concentrating on the task.

Another criterion for PMDD is that it cannot be merely an increase in severity of another disorder's symptoms (such as a mood disorder, panic disorder, or a personality disorder). PMDD may trigger a panic attack or some other symptom of another disorder, but its symptoms must be charted for at least two menstrual cycles, so that the symptoms can be seen to cluster around menstruation.

Although the monthly hormone cycle causes its own problems, these changes have been known to induce attacks of chronic problems to women suffering from epilepsy, connective tissue diseases (such

# Premenstrual Magnification

Some researchers believe that PMS can cause other emotional or physical problems to become more severe during the last part of the luteal phase. For example, those suffering from eating disorders such as bulimia, a disorder in which the sufferer binges on food and then purges it (or vomits), may have an increase in bingeing during this time. Alcoholics or other substance abusers may use drugs or alcohol more, while those who suffer from anxiety disorders may have a greater number of attacks during this time. Even asthma and herpes sufferers often experience a sudden intensification of their symptoms.

hypoglycemia: An abnormal decrease in the level of sugar in the body.

colitis: Inflammation of the colon.

as systemic lupus erythematosus, fibromyalgia, and arthritis), hypoglycemia, colitis, and asthma.

For women who are affected each month by fluctuating hormone levels, understanding PMS by identifying the symptoms and how they relate to the menstrual cycle may be the first step in gaining relief. Experiencing the onslaught of both physical and emotional upheaval for up to two weeks can have an alarming effect on a woman's life and the lives of those around her. Until recently, these symptoms have been overlooked by the medical world. Today, however, medications can help sufferers live normally all month long.

As Emily writes in her diary, her world changes once a month. She can't understand herself or those around her. She is more volatile, argues with her friends and family. Schoolwork is more difficult, and she sometimes feels physically ill and cannot face the rigors of

PMS can cause other problems to get worse. In other words, if a young woman has a mood disorder, her depression will likely be worse during the time each month when she experiences hormonal changes.

What a woman eats and drinks can influence her PMS symptoms.

# Some PMS Facts

- Even though estrogen, which has an impact on brain chemicals by affecting moods and energy levels, is high during the first half of the menstrual cycle and progesterone, which seems to overpower these same brain chemicals, is high during the last half of the cycle, there is no proof that the hormones directly affect PMS symptoms. In fact, when women are tested they have normal hormone levels.
- If women do not treat PMS symptoms, they often get worse.
- Some women experience symptoms at the time of ovulation for just a day or two and then have a week with no symptoms at all, followed by PMS disturbances the week or two before their menses start.
- Caffeine is a major problem in PMS symptoms. Coffee and chocolate are the major offenders, but caffeine is also found in soft drinks and tea.
- The largest group of women who seek treatment for the symptoms of PMS are between the ages of 30 and 40; they are usually mothers of two or more children.
- If your mother has PMS, you are more likely to suffer from PMS symptoms.
- Many women report that their PMS symptoms worsen with age.
- Depressed women and those with other mental illnesses are more likely to suffer, and the symptoms of their illness are more likely to be aggravated.
- Sometimes after pelvic surgery, ovarian surgery, or a hysterectomy, PMS symptoms worsen.

# A Sample Chart

| | Month 1 | Month 2 | Month 3 |
|---|---|---|---|
| 1 | | | |
| 2 | | | |
| 3 | | | |
| 4 | | | |
| 5 | | | |
| 6 | | | |
| 7 | | | |
| 8 | | | |
| 9 | | | |
| 10 | | | |
| 11 | | | |
| 12 | | | |
| 13 | | | |
| 14 | | | |
| 15 | | | |
| 16 | | | |
| 17 | | | |
| 18 | | | |
| 19 | | | |
| 20 | | | |
| 21 | | | |
| 22 | | | |
| 23 | | | |
| 24 | | | |
| 25 | | | |
| 26 | | | |
| 27 | | | |
| 28 | | | |
| 29 | | | |
| 30 | | | |
| 31 | | | |

Record your symptoms for three consecutive menstrual cycles on the chart to the left, using the letters to represent the symptom you are experiencing. If the symptom is mild to moderate use a lower case letter, but if it is severe record a capital letter. Use an "M" to mark your menstrual flow days.

H — Headache
BT — Breast Tenderness
I — Irritability
B — Backache
O — Outbursts of Temper
IA — Increased Appetite
HP — Heart Palpitations

F — Food Cravings
T — Tired
S — Sleeplessness
A — Anxiety
D — Dizziness
AB — Abdominal Bloating

If you experience symptoms other than these, add them and a corresponding letter to this list and chart them also.

her everyday schedule. Even her clothes fit differently than at other times of the month. Emily's mother notices the changes and feels they are severe enough that Emily should see her physician. Emily, with the help of her physician, will need to learn the truth about menstrual symptoms and how this natural and important cycle affects her moods and her body before she can live more normally.

A young woman who is experiencing PMS symptoms may feel withdrawn and irritable. If her symptoms are severe enough, medication may be an option she will want to consider.

# Chapter Two

# History of Zoloft and Prozac

Emily Palmer's Journal, September 30

*I'm so tired of everyone thinking there's something wrong with me. Mom keeps getting on my case, reminding me that I have to fill out this chart that the doctor gave me. I have to write in when I have a headache, when I'm tired, if I have increased appetite, and my favorite—when I have breast tenderness. Just what I want the world to know about me. Besides, I feel great. My test in chemistry yesterday went so good. I knew everything. I hope I get a 100. That will show them all. It's been almost two weeks and I haven't gotten to talk to Sarah about everything. It's really taking her a long time to*

In the nineteenth century, few doctors took women's monthly symptoms seriously. Women were expected to be weak and prone to emotional "vapors."

*get over our fight. It wasn't that big, I mean I hardly remember what happened, and I told her I was sorry that I lost it. We finally went out to our favorite sub shop for lunch today, and I treated. I'm excited about our Homecoming Dance next month. We're both going, Sarah with Cory and me with Mark. Mark and Cory are best friends just like Sarah and me, so it should be fun. And this weekend we go shopping for our dresses. I can't wait.*

Emily's having a great week. She's in her second week of her cycle, her menses are over, and things are looking fine—but unfortunately, she hasn't figured out yet that her good feelings will only last for another week or so.

Even though it will take her time to figure out exactly how her body is reacting to hormones and other changes that happen during her monthly cycle, Emily and others like her have the benefit of today's research. Scientists who look to affect changes in imbalances in the body have led the way to the development of drugs that help normalize the extreme symptoms of PMS and PMDD.

syndrome: A group of signs and symptoms that occur together and characterize a particular abnormality.

As long ago as 450 BC, Hippocrates may have been one of the first researchers to notice the effects of premenstrual symptoms. But from then until very recently, the cyclical effects on women each month did not receive the effort needed to cause any major changes in treatment or recognition of PMS as a real syndrome.

As recently as 1931, R. T. Frank described the symptoms women experience monthly as premenstrual tension. Finally, in 1953, Dr. Katharina Dalton studied the symptoms and the way they affect women each month. She believed there was a real link between the monthly cycle and the physical and psychological symptoms. Dr. Dalton began looking for ways to treat this disorder. She was the first to use the term premenstrual syndrome to describe the pattern of symptoms. And she began an almost one-woman campaign to not

## Facts about Selective Serotonin Reuptake Inhibitors

- Since their introduction in 1988, the SSRI antidepressants have become the most widely used antidepressants.
- SSRIs were specifically designed for help with treating depression. Unlike many medications, they were not found accidentally while trying to find something else.
- Unlike some other antidepressants, SSRIs are not addictive.
- Because they change the way the brain works, which can be different for each person, individual SSRIs do not change one person's symptoms the same way they do another's. Sometimes those who take antidepressants must try more than one before they find the medication that works best for them.
- At least fourteen subtypes of serotonin exist, which could lead to the development of even more specific drugs that will act on these serotonin subtypes.

only prove that PMS existed but that there were ways it could be treated to normalize women's lives.

Although there has been widespread belief that most cases of PMS can be treated with diet, exercise, and even diuretics, there are those like Emily who are unable to function each month with all of these changes. Even though she is careful about what she eats (except when she can't control her cravings) and exercises regularly, Emily still suffers. Women like her need more help, and for them antidepressants have often been able to change their lives. Christiane Northrup, M.D., in her book *Women's Bodies, Women's Wisdom*, says she always advises women to make lifestyle changes

Eating plenty of fruits and vegetables may help make a woman more healthy and better able to cope with her hormonal fluctuations. But for some women, diet alone is not enough to control their premenstrual mood swings. Psychiatric medication may offer them another option.

such as diet, exercise, vitamins, and progesterone therapy. "But," Dr. Northrup emphasizes, "in persistent cases of PMS, a deeper imbalance exists that lifestyle changes alone won't help." In the more severe cases of PMS and PMDD, physicians have found that altering the brain chemistry by using antidepressants helps to relieve symptoms. (See chapter three.)

When iproniazid, one of the first antidepressants, was originally studied, it was used to treat tuberculosis. In the early 1950s, physicians noticed that their patients treated with the drug became more

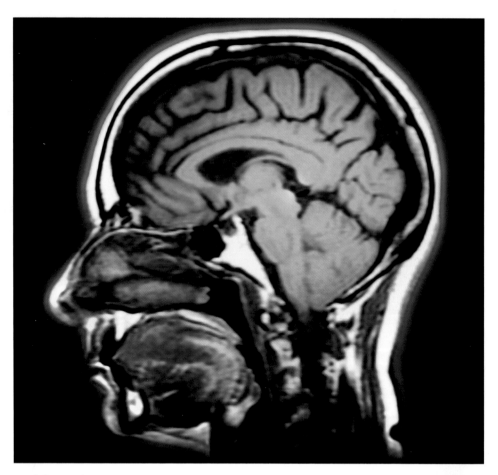

Although an MRI allows researchers to examine the brain's complicated structure, scientists are still struggling to fully understand how the brain works.

In the June 20, 2002, issue of *Women's Health Weekly*, the magazine reported that the United States Food and Drug Administration had approved the use of Zoloft for the treatment of PMDD. In an experiment composed of women with and without premenstrual syndrome, both groups were given a drug that temporarily suppresses sex hormones and the reproductive cycle. Before the drug was taken, both groups had the same female hormone levels and the same hormonal activity during the entire menstrual cycle. But when the drug was administered, the women with PMS or PMDD were symptom free; only when they took estrogen or progesterone did the symptoms return. The women who had no PMS previously remained the same. So even though the hormone levels remained consistent, those who suffer from PMS and PMDD must be sensitive to hormone fluctuations. It may be that the hormone's effects on the brain cause the problems. Studies are beginning to show serotonin fluctuations in women who suffer from PMS, but more especially those suffering from PMDD. That is why antidepressants like Zoloft work to help alleviate the symptoms.

Another study of identical twins showed that if one identical twin experienced PMDD, 90 percent of the other twins also suffered with PMDD, compared with 44 percent of fraternal twins and only 31 percent of sisters who were not twins. Because of studies like this, researchers are looking for variations in genes that code for serotonin.

Adapted from "Premenstrual Mood Disturbance," *Harvard Mental Health Letter,* June 2001.

energetic and elevated in mood, even though their tuberculosis was not improving. These happier patients led researchers to evaluate the drug more carefully to find if it had any effect on those suffering from depression.

Treating depressed patients with iproniazid became prevalent after a 1957 article stated that research showed its ability to improve the symptoms of this distressing mental illness. Even though the drug enjoyed such immediate success, soon after the widespread use of iproniazid began the fear of side effects caused the manufacturer to take it off the market.

sedative: Something that has a calming, soothing effect.

Meanwhile, Ronald Kuhn, a leading researcher in Switzerland, was looking for a specific drug to fight depression that would be nonstimulating in its action, so that the person would feel better but not be specifically energized or agitated. Kuhn began by studying antihistamines. (The antihistamine chlorpromazine hydrochloride was already being used to treat schizophrenia.) As a sedative chlorpromazine had a calming effect but only a fair amount of success when treating depression. It seemed that just calming the patient did not alleviate the major symptoms of depression.

By the end of 1957, Kuhn announced the discovery of a substance that would relieve depression. This drug was called imipramine and was the first of the antidepressants specifically designed to treat depression without overstimulating the recipient. Once they began using this drug, patients' appetites returned and they became more like themselves. But most important, they experienced no abnormal elevation of mood; in fact, when nondepressed persons took imipramine, they simply became sedated. This meant the drug would have little chance of becoming addictive.

Norepinephrine and serotonin are two neurotransmitters, chemicals that carry messages between brain cells. Because the antidepressant imipramine affected both serotonin and norepi-

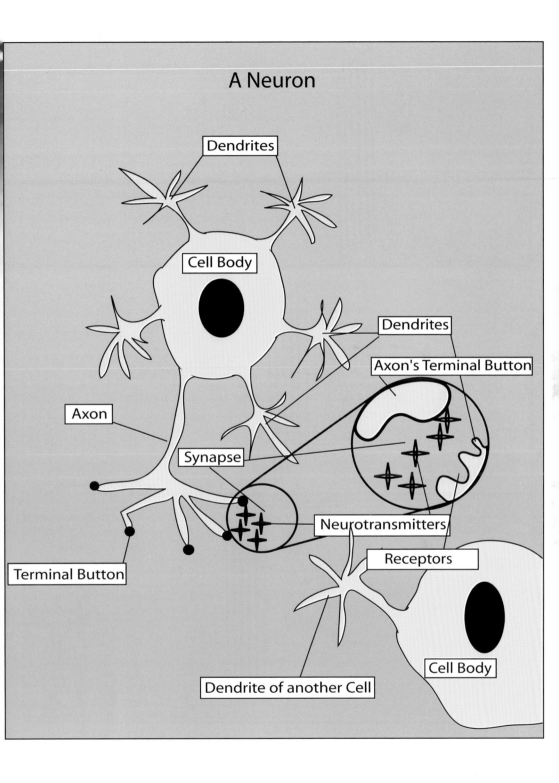

A Neuron

Adrenaline causes the "fight-or-flight" reaction.

nephrine transmitters, it was less effective. Treating neurotransmitters that did not need to be treated caused unnecessary side effects. The more parts of the body altered by a medication, the greater the number of side effects. Some of imipramine's side effects—sweating, heart palpitations, dry mouth, blurry vision, and difficulty in urinating—were caused by the body reacting as if it was in an emergency situation. Just as if a tiger was stalking it in the jungle, the patient's body was ready to run or to fight at any time. The need for a drug with fewer side effects was still apparent.

homology: A similarity attributable to a common origin.

analogy: A resemblance to some characteristics between things that are otherwise unlike.

hypertension: High blood pressure.

When drugs are discovered that have a desired effect but have some problem side effects as well, researchers continue their search for a better alternative by creating similar chemicals. This type of research is called homology, because the researchers use the fundamental structure of the original chemical but try to change some part of the formula. Because this is the easiest route toward a desired goal, much research starts here.

New drugs may also be developed using analogy. In this case, researchers look for substances that will function similarly. In other words, if they have an antidepressant that affects the brain by influencing the levels of available serotonin, they look for other substance structures that will do the same thing.

Like the first antidepressants, monoamine oxidase inhibitors (MAOIs) worked well when treating depression. Although researchers have proven that these drugs inhibit monoamine oxidase that works in the neurons of the brain, exactly how the drugs work is not known. If the patient has hypertension, MAOIs need to be used with much caution. This meant that the drug's use was limited for many patients. Research continued for yet another alternative.

Imipramine is called tricyclic because its chemical structure looks like three rings. Once scientists realized that imipramine worked to combat depression, researchers looked for other molecules that had three chemical rings, an example of homology.

Many researchers, however, still believed that serotonin held the key to most mood problems. Although another new antidepressant called desipramine was developed, it affected the transmitter nor-epinephrine more than serotonin—and so the search for a drug that affected only serotonin continued.

Finally, in the 1960s, Bryan Molloy, a Scottish chemist, and Ray Fuller, a pharmacologist, working together at Eli Lilly and Company, a pharmaceutical researching and manufacturing firm, used a combination of studies to find the first selective serotonin reuptake inhibitors (SSRIs). Molloy was working on a heart regulator, while Fuller was testing new antidepressants on rats. Fuller convinced Molloy to work on chemicals that affect transmitters in the brain. Molloy began by studying previous work on neurotransmitters. Because much of this work had been done using antihistamines, Molloy decided to start with them, using a model by a third researcher at Lilly, Robert Rathbun. Finally, David Wong, a researcher in antibiotics, began studying the role of serotonin in mood regulation. Together, this team searched for answers to the serotonin problem in mood regulation.

When Wong learned of the research of Solomon Snyder of Johns Hopkins University, he began using his technology on Molloy's antidepressants. He quickly found that they were like drugs already available. He continued his research by testing the chemicals that had failed Molloy's tests. One of these, a compound labeled 82816, was found to block the uptake of serotonin without affecting other transmitters. The test was run on Fuller's rats next. From these studies, Bryan Molloy and Klaus Schmiegel, another Lilly researcher, co-invented a group of synthesized compounds called aryloxphenylpropylamines, which includes the compound called fluoxetine oxalate. These chemicals were then made into fluoxetine hydrochloride, the active ingredient in Prozac.

# Drug Approval

Before a drug can be marketed in the United States, it must be officially approved by the Food and Drug Administration (FDA). Today's FDA is the primary consumer protection agency in the United States. Operating under the authority given it by the government, and guided by laws established throughout the twentieth century, the FDA has established a rigorous drug approval process that verifies the safety, effectiveness, and accuracy of labeling for any drug marketed in the United States.

While the United States has the FDA for the approval and regulation of drugs and medical devices, Canada has a similar organization called the Therapeutic Product Directorate (TPD). The TPD is a division of Health Canada, the Canadian government department of health. The TPD regulates drugs, medical devices, disinfectants, and santizers with disinfectant claims. Some of the things that the TPD monitors are quality, effectiveness, and safety. Just as the FDA must approve new drugs in the United States, the TPD must approve new drugs in Canada before those drugs can enter the market.

Prozac was introduced in 1988, about thirty years after the first antidepressants became available. Because of its specific effect on serotonin, Prozac offered relatively few side effects. Previous problems with the heart were not likely with Prozac, and patients did not feel lethargic or sedated.

Zoloft (sertraline hydrochloride) and the other SSRIs were developed after Prozac. Although these drugs do have side effects, these are less severe than those of the antidepressants that were developed before them. For those suffering from depression, the drugs are able to change serotonin levels and affect the brain positively.

## Brand Name vs. Generic

Talking about psychiatric drugs can be confusing, because every drug has at least two names: its "generic name" and the "brand name" that the pharmaceutical company uses to market the drug. Generic names come from the drugs' chemical structures, while drug companies use brand names to inspire consumers' recognition and loyalty.

Zoloft and Prozac are brand names; their generic names are sertraline hydrochloride and fluoxetine hydrochloride.

Eventually, researchers discovered that those who experienced symptoms of PMS gained relief from these drugs.

When Kim first saw her physician, she was suffering more from the results of her poor relationships than from the symptoms of PMS, or so she thought. She had just had a huge argument with her husband that had ended with Kim packing all his clothes and fishing gear and taking them to his mother's house. She was done with him.

She had also screamed at her children all day long. That night, she hated being at home alone with them. Her husband had begged to come home, but she insisted he was the cause of all her problems; she was not going to put up with his selfish fishing and his long work hours.

After her visit to her doctor, Kim learned she had a monthly chemical imbalance in her brain. Like Emily, Kim's monthly cycle was affecting the rest of her life. She recognized that she didn't always feel her husband was unreasonable; in fact, most of the time she thought he was very considerate. He always helped with the house and did his share of taking care of the children. Kim made the important discovery that her husband's behavior seemed worse once a month, whenever she was experiencing the symptoms of PMS.

Kim made another discovery that was even more important: she did not have to live with the emotional and chemical imbalances caused by her menstrual cycle. Instead, she could use one of the SSRI antidepressants and live peacefully all month.

Young women who are experiencing PMS symptoms will find that their emotional outlooks change from week to week. If their depression is severe enough, psychiatric drugs called SSRIs may offer them some relief.

# Chapter Three

# How Do SSRIs Work?

E mily Palmer's Journal, January 7

I can't believe it's been more than three months since I first started this stupid chart. I hate doing it, but I am starting to see what the doctor means. There is this group of days each month when I feel terrible and I mark lots of symptoms during that time—then I get my period and like wow, I feel better.

I'm beginning to think I like getting my period. All that mess that I used to hate now seems like a relief. Boy, it was too bad I didn't have it when Sarah and I went to the Homecoming Dance. I think it was about three days before my period and my dress (that had fit me just fine when I bought it) was too tight. I looked like I had poured myself into it. I'm sure that whole bag of cookies I ate the night before didn't *help. I tried not to eat so many. I said to myself, "One cookie, just one." But then I ate another and another and another. . . oh, why did I do it? And, of course, Mom came in as I was eating the last one. She got really mad, especially cause she has been trying so hard to get me to eat more healthy.*

*And then the dance—yuck! I tried to be so careful about what I said and did, but everything seemed to go wrong. The guys were late so we had to rush eating dinner to get to the dance on time. All I told Sarah was that they could have been a little more considerate. But of course she thought I was blaming it all on Cory since he was the one who drove, and then she got mad because I was criticizing him. But I mean, we don't get to go out like that every week! I guess I did say it kind of loud, though. Oh, and when I asked Cory where he learned to drive, like maybe at racing school, he didn't take it too well. But I thought he was flying, and so I told him either he better drive slower or I'd report him. I mean Sarah should be happy I didn't want her to get hurt. What kind of friend would I be if I just ignored his speeding?*

*And then my back was so sore with my period I didn't think I'd be able to walk the next day. Maybe there's something really wrong with me. Sarah doesn't seem to get like me when she has her period. Well, I guess I'll wait a little longer.*

*I go to the doctor next week and he'll look at all this chart stuff and maybe he'll do something. At least I hope he can do something before I lose my best friend. I don't know what I'd do without Sarah.*

Researchers are beginning to think that women like Emily may suffer from fluctuating serotonin levels during their menstrual cycles. These fluctuating levels may be what cause their symptoms, including Emily's anger, weight gain, cravings, and other experiences. Because not enough serotonin transmitters are getting to the receptors, messages are not getting passed from cell to cell as needed. Women who binge by eating too much chocolate or too many sugary desserts may be suffering from low serotonin levels. If they had more serotonin, they'd be able to recognize and fight urges like these.

A woman may feel bloated and achy during and before her menstrual period.

neurons: Nerve cells.

Antidepressants affect the way the brain functions as it sends messages throughout the nervous system by way of neurons. Each message your brain sends moves from neuron to neuron. The neurons are not connected; in fact, a small gap, called a synapse, lies between each neuron. Messages move across the gaps by way of chemicals called neurotransmitters. Neurotransmitters, once their job of relaying the message is accomplished, are partially broken down and sent as waste to the kidneys. The remaining neurons are reabsorbed into the nerve by a process called reuptake.

Serotonin is just one of the neurotransmitters that relay messages within the brain, but it is the one that affects our moods and emotions. By forcing the neurotransmitter to remain in the synapse

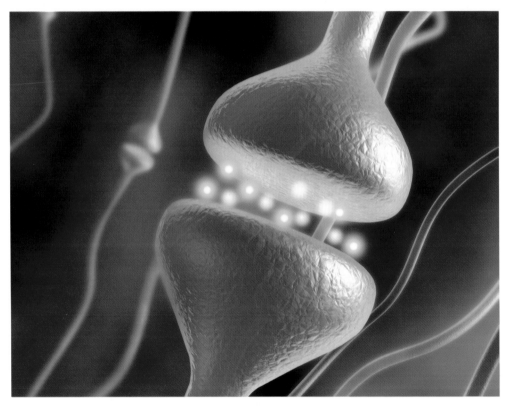

Neurotransmitters moving across the synapse between two neurons.

The human brain is an amazing and complex organ. It comprises only about two percent of the body's weight, and yet it helps control and regulate the entire body. As a part of the central nervous system, the brain coordinates the sensory information experienced by the body, allowing it to react to or process this stimulation. It also directs automatic functions in the body such as the heartbeat and respiration. It releases hormones and controls body temperature, hunger, and pleasure.

longer, the brain has more serotonin at its disposal as it sends messages. To accomplish this, reuptake needs to be inhibited to some extent.

Scientists began their research looking for a drug that would cause what they thought was a malfunctioning serotonin system to work correctly. As their research progressed, however, scientists came to believe that some individuals are simply more sensitive to the serotonin levels within their brains. When the brain has an ample supply of serotonin, messages are transmitted properly between nerve cells and emotional symptoms are alleviated. But "an ample supply of serotonin" may be different for different people.

The antidepressants called SSRIs cause only the transmitter serotonin to be inhibited from the reuptake phase. Antidepressants such as Zoloft and Prozac are from the SSRI group. They are able to change the brain's chemistry by keeping only serotonin from being reabsorbed within the brain. By making sure that more serotonin is available within the brain, many of the symptoms of depression are eliminated.

Lower levels of serotonin may cause erratic eating like Emily's, because the brain will do what it needs to raise the serotonin level. First, it will open more receptors to grab as many serotonin transmitters as it can find; if that doesn't work, the brain may produce food cravings. This is what can lead to eating whole bags of choco-

People who have a low serotonin level may experience:

- less intense moods
- depression
- aggression
- increased risk of heart disease
- anxiety
- poor concentration
- impulsive behavior
- feelings of guilt
- food cravings
- alcoholism
- anger and/or rage

late cookies (and other foods) in order to try to raise serotonin levels through food intake. Studies show that carbohydrates cause serotonin levels to increase.

Researchers, however, still do not completely understand the relationship between serotonin and mood. Lower serotonin levels can make people depressed; these people may also experience anxiety, forgetfulness, and other PMS symptoms. Those women who do not suffer from these symptoms do not have extremely high levels of serotonin, only normal levels. Some women may even have low serotonin levels and yet never experience any PMS symptoms.

SSRI antidepressants work to regulate the brain's available levels of serotonin transmitters. But they can help alleviate many symptoms, not just depression, anxiety, and other mood imbalances. Anything that happens within the brain affects the whole body. The brain's complex network is like a computer, where everything the body experiences is processed and saved. The brain also directs each move the body makes. That's why when one part of the body experiences bloating or pain, the brain sends information that causes the body to react. Serotonin levels affect the way the entire body functions.

A person with low serotonin levels may feel depressed.

Low serotonin levels may cause chocolate cravings.

Ample serotonin helps a person feel calm and relaxed. It also increases control over impulses. A woman experiencing PMS may want to eat a doughnut for breakfast and then a chocolate candy bar for a snack, when normally she eats cereal for breakfast and an apple for a snack. Because of her low serotonin levels, she is not only experiencing cravings for carbohydrates she is probably suffering from poor impulse control and her thinking may be less clear and rational than usual.

SSRIs prevent serotonin from moving into the nerve endings. By doing this, the serotonin is forced to remain in the spaces surrounding nerve endings, allowing the serotonin to act on them. The medication does not produce more serotonin; instead it is the serotonin that is altered. This action is what affects the mood level in disorders like PMDD.

SSRIs also increase mental alertness, physical activity, and can even allow the user to sleep better, which also affects aspects of PMDD. Unlike tranquilizers that work to slow the body by calming it, SSRIs act as regulators. In the same way that your thermostat in your home keeps the temperature constant, these drugs work to keep serotonin at a productive level within the brain. They accomplish this without making the patient too lethargic and sleepy to accomplish everyday tasks.

By increasing the levels of serotonin in the brain, researchers have found there is an increase in confidence and a sense of well-being. Serotonin may also affect how a person feels pain: the more serotonin, the less pain. Also, the more serotonin, the less fear and anger. Researchers have found that within monkey societies, the animal with the most serotonin in the brain and nervous system was the highest leader within the community. The most insecure monkeys had the lowest serotonin levels.

Now that Emily and her doctor have the information to make a diagnosis, they can better understand her behaviors. There are physical, chemical reasons for Emily's craving for an entire bag of chocolate cookies when two weeks ago she would never think of eating so

A young woman who is experiencing PMS symptoms may consume an entire box of chocolate. SSRIs can help control her food binges and mood swings.

much. Understanding at what point she is in her menstrual cycle will help both her and her doctor decide what steps to take next. If she feels she can't control her mood swings and bingeing, she, her mother, and her physician may decide that Emily needs the help of one of the SSRI antidepressants to regulate her serotonin levels. These drugs may give her the ability to better live her life the way she wants.

Medication is often an effective treatment for depression caused by PMS—but it can also be expensive.

# Chapter Four

# Treatment Using SSRIs

E mily Palmer's Journal, February 18

Well, I guess that doctor has had some experience with this premenstrual stuff. He loaded me up with all kinds of information, and I'm going to try taking an antidepressant. Not that I like taking medicine, but he really thinks this is going to help me. He wants me to take it only for the last two weeks before I get my period; he thinks it will help me not to feel like I'm going crazy. Since I'm feeling okay the rest of the month, I don't have to take any medicine then.

I think I can live with this. Especially if it helps me and my temper. I really can't believe that I'm fine for a couple weeks and then I can't even control myself. I had such a big argument with Dad last week that I'm grounded for a month. I didn't even mean the stuff I said.

Not every woman who experiences PMS needs to take a psychiatric medication—but for those whose symptoms are severe, psychiatric drugs may offer hope and healing.

*I wonder if he'll take away my punishment once Mom tells him the doctor thinks I have no control over this. After all, it was his fault for getting me so mad, wasn't it?*

*But then again, maybe it wasn't Dad's fault. The doctor sent me to see a therapist, Dr. Jill, and she talked to me about choices and stuff. I guess she said my choices are my own and I am responsible for them. I can't blame what I do on somebody else. My actions don't have to be based on what Sarah or Dad or anybody else says but on what I know is right. Each time I explode, I always think someone else has made me do it. But no matter what time of the month it is, I have control over my own words, no one else does.*

*This may take some getting used to. Sometimes it just seems too hard. But if I ignore what Dr. Jill and the doctor tell me, then I'll have to continue like I am now. I don't want that. I hate being grounded, I hate fighting with my best friend, and I hate feeling like I can't even think straight. I could go crazy if I go on like this.*

When Emily takes her first antidepressant she will be using one of the SSRIs approved by the U.S. Food and Drug Administration to help control the symptoms of PMS and its more serious cousin, PMDD.

As the medicine enters the bloodstream, it travels to the brain and attaches itself to the serotonin neurotransmitters, helping the signals of the brain to be stronger and more normal. This allows the brain to signal other parts of the body properly, protecting it from pain, headaches, tension, and other annoying symptoms that are part of the monthly struggles of PMS sufferers.

On November 3, 1999, the Food and Drug Administration's Psychopharmacologic Advisory Committee recommended that fluoxetine hydrochloride, the main ingredient in Prozac, be approved to treat women with PMDD. They advised that the drug be used only for women whose symptoms are severe enough to cause problems while at work, school, or during social activities. Without the drug, these women would not be able to function at the same level during the week or two they experience symptoms as they would the rest of the month. As a result of this recommendation, Eli Lilly, manu-

# Precautions for taking Zoloft and Prozac

1. Always inform your doctor of any other medications, prescription or over-the-counter, that you are taking.

2. Consuming alcoholic beverages is not recommended.

3. Caution should be taken when using:
   - Tagamet, ulcer treatment
   - Diazipam, anti-anxiety and sedative treatment
   - Digitoxin, heart treatment
   - Lithium, manic-depressive and bipolar treatment
   - Other psychiatric antidepressants such as Elavil and Mellaril
   - Over-the-counter cold remedies
   - Tolbutamide, hypoglycemic treatment
   - Warfarin, an anticoagulant

4. Serious and potentially fatal reactions can occur when taking an MAOI such as Nardil, Parnate, and Marplan. Allow fourteen days between discontinuing MAOI therapy and beginning Zoloft or Prozac.

5. A rash can be the sign of a serious medical condition for those taking Prozac. See your physician immediately if you develop a rash while taking the medication.

6. Alert your physician of any reactions to other antidepressants.

Pychiatric drugs cannot be taken lightly or casually. It is important to follow the prescribing practitioner's instructions exactly, in order to avoid potentially dangerous side effects.

facturer of Prozac, decided to repackage and rename Prozac for the women's market. The new name, Sarafem, with its pink and purple pills, was ready to help women who feel out of control for one to two weeks a month bring normalcy back to their lives. In July 2000, the FDA finally acted on the recommendation and approved Sarafem to treat PMDD.

Sarafem is usually taken once a day, in the morning, and should be taken close to the same time every day. A missed pill must be taken within a few hours or that dose should be skipped. Doses should never be doubled to make up for a missed dose. The prescription should be stored at room temperature. The patient's doctor should be kept informed of any changes—good or bad—that the patient experiences while taking Sarafem.

The FDA bases its approval on specific research results. Sometimes, a particular use for a drug may have been thoroughly researched by many studies, while other uses lack the same amount of research. In that case, the drug label will only include the uses that have met the FDA's stringent research requirements. Physicians, however, may continue to prescribe that drug for other "off-label" uses.

# Dosages

Prozac can be started with a 20-milligram dose but should not exceed 80 milligrams per day. Those eighteen and younger are often prescribed a dose between 5 milligrams and 40 milligrams. For those who have mild feelings of anxiety, one pill can be taken every other day. This causes no problem because the medication remains in the body for several days.

When treating depression, some patients may notice an improvement of symptoms within two weeks, but most will need as much as four weeks. When treating PMDD or PMS, however, the results of treatment are in many cases immediate. Emily may begin to feel a difference the first month that she takes the medication.

Those who have trouble sleeping while taking Prozac should take their dose in the morning. This is sometimes the only adjustment needed to alleviate this problem.

Zoloft is another of the SSRIs approved for treating PMDD. It can be taken either every day of the month or for the two weeks prior to the onset of menstruation. The usual starting dosage for adults taking Zoloft is 50 milligrams once a day, either in the morning or the evening. For those having a problem with insomnia, Zoloft should be taken in the morning. It is available in 25-milligram, 50-milligram, and 100-milligram scored tablets that can be divided to allow adjustment of dosages. Those who are sensitive to medications should start out at 25 milligrams, which can then be raised after a week or

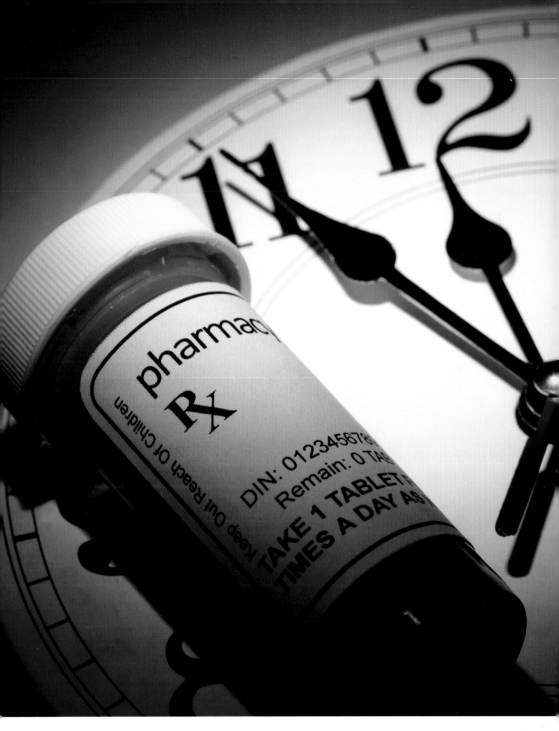

Many psychiatric medications should be taken at the same time each day.

more of treatment but should not exceed 200 milligrams per day. A dose may be crushed and mixed with food or left in tablet form. Taking Zoloft without food will not upset the stomach, but food does enhance absorption.

Like Prozac, Zoloft takes about four weeks before the depressed patient feels the full effect of the medication, and it can take up to eight weeks for some individuals. But a woman suffering from PMDD may notice significant changes within the first cycle after she begins taking the drug. The lowest possible effective dose is recommended.

Follow dosage instructions exactly when taking any medication.

At a British boarding school, the faculty recorded in discipline books the dates and reasons girls were disciplined. They also kept a book recording when girls signed that they needed sanitary protection. By comparing the books, the faculty could see that immediately before and during menstruation there were twice as many disciplinary problems as otherwise. Offenses included forgetfulness, tardiness, and irritability. There also seemed to be a slow reaction time, so things like talking in class were disciplined more often before and during their menstrual periods. (If a teacher entered the room, those with a slower reaction time did not realize it soon enough and were caught talking.) Another interesting fact was that teacher's helpers, those who were allowed to discipline fellow students to help keep order in the classroom, gave more disciplinary punishments during their own menstruations than any other time of the month.

Adapted from *Once a Month* by Katharina Dalton, M.D.

Because of this, a physician will start the woman on a lower dose and increase it only if the symptoms are ongoing.

If a dose of Zoloft is missed, it must be taken as soon as possible. If, however, several hours have passed, the dose should be skipped, as no one should ever take a double dose. The pills are best stored at room temperature. As with Prozac, the physician should always be informed of any changes that the person experiences, good or bad, while taking Zoloft.

Studies that compare women who take antidepressants continuously with women who take them only during their luteal phase have found that those medicated during the luteal phase reported the same results as those who took the drug as a continuous daily dose. Because of this study, many physicians advocate the use of the drug only intermittently instead of continuously. The benefits of this

# Who can diagnose a psychiatric disorder?

- psychiatrists
- psychiatric advanced practice nurses
- medical doctors
- clinical nurse specialists
- nurse psychiatrists
- social workers
- psychologists

However, in most of the United States only medical doctors, psychiatrists, clinical nurse specialists, nurse psychiatrists, and advanced practice nurses can prescribe psychotropic medication.

tolerance: The capacity of the body to endure or become less responsive to a substance (as a drug) or a physiological insult with repeated use or exposure.

treatment schedule could be decreased side effects and a longer drug tolerance.

One of the most important precautions to remember about taking Zoloft or Prozac is that there can be a very dangerous or fatal reaction between these drugs and MAOIs. If you are presently taking any of the MAOIs—drugs such as Nardil, Parnate, and Marplan—or have quit taking one within the past two weeks, do not begin taking Zoloft or Prozac without telling your physician about your drug history.

Many researchers have studied the effectiveness and safety of Prozac and Zoloft. The drugs are now considered safe to use but must be monitored by a doctor regularly, because each person reacts differently to medication. Some people are so sensitive they

A psychiatric advanced practice nurse is just one professional who can diagnose and treat a psychiatric disorder.

need to decrease their dosages. It is always best to start at very low levels, moving slowly up to the lowest effective dose.

Most studies are done on women, not adolescents. Many adults assume all teenagers will rebel and act out during these years, so they do not consider that some teenage girls may be suffering from PMS or PMDD rather than just being rebellious. One mother reported to a friend, "If you think you had trouble with your son, wait until your daughter becomes a teenager. They are ten times worse than any boy." Many physicians who treat adolescents, however, are coming to believe that a close association may exist between a young woman's behavior and her menstrual cycle. Girls who were well-behaved and pleasant children may suddenly become distant,

# How to Manage PMS Before It Starts

- Plan around PMS symptoms. Try to make appointments, take classes, and plan vacations around your monthly schedule. This includes dinner parties, extended shopping trips, and having overnight guests.

- Don't make any major decisions while you are having PMS symptoms. Keep a calendar handy with your cycle marked. Don't change jobs or end relationships. When you feel the most frustrated, write down the problem and deal with it after your period.

- Remind your family of your PMS difficulties. Share when you will experience the most problems and ask for help. Tell them to gently remind you that this is something that will pass and urge them to support your efforts to be as normal as possible during that time.

- Take good care of yourself throughout your cycle so that you feel your best at the end of it. Nap, rest, read, take a walk, do what you need to help yourself so that you are a positive influence on those around you.

Medication offers an appropriate treatment for premenstrual disorders—but it is no magic genie in a bottle!

secretive, and moody. When they act out for two weeks a month, they may give others the impression that their true personality is troublesome. But these girls may be trapped by their symptoms. They desperately need someone to understand.

One young woman dropped out of school, went from job to job, and ignored her family; her mother only began to see the correlation between her daughter's behavior and her menstrual cycle after she found the young woman hunched over in a corner suffering from an overdose of drugs. After seeking help—and getting treatment for her PMDD—the young woman went back to school at night and started her life over.

When young women like Emily get the appropriate treatment, it may cause major changes in their lives. For the first time, they may have the freedom to do and be all that they want to be.

Psychiatric drugs can help a young woman with severe PMS symptoms regain a happier, more balanced outlook on life.

# Chapter Five

# Case Studies

Emily Palmer's Journal, March 14

Well, I've been taking the antidepressant for almost a month and things are going so much better. I never noticed that people, even teachers, avoided me during certain times of the month. Sarah and I joke about that now. She teases me about the strange looks I get every so often from someone now when I'm talking and smiling at them. When I ask her what's going on, she tells me I always fought with those girls. It's almost like I was this alien or something.

Now that I think about it, I know how lucky I was to have Sarah to help me. I know she must have tried to make me look good as much as she could. And boy, some kids must have thought she was nuts hanging around with me. But she stuck with me, I guess because we've known each other since we were little, and she hoped I'd come around or something. I hope I'm as good a friend to her if she ever needs me.

The doctor is happy with my report of the month, but he still wants me to watch what I eat and see Dr. Jill once a month for a while. I don't mind because I like learning about myself. I especially like that Dr. Jill has taught me to stop when I get angry and **RETHINK**. This means I:

- **R**ecognize my anger.
- Have **E**mpathy for the other person (try to walk in his or her shoes sort of).
- **T**hink about what I am angry about in a different way. Maybe I could see something funny or even try to solve the problem rather than just be angry.
- **H**ear the other person; don't just think about myself, tuning out everybody else.
- **I**ntegrate love and respect. I can tell the person how I feel about the situation instead of blaming or putting her down.
- **N**otice what works for me. How do I control my anger the best? I think maybe I need space for a little while when I'm feeling frustrated. But that doesn't mean I should go over the whole thing in my mind and work myself up even more; instead, I should just let it go for a while.
- **K**eep my focus on the present. This I really need to work on. I'm always reminding myself and everybody else about old problems, as if they will make anything better now. I hope I can continue to do this because I've already seen it work when I try it.

Emily's change at school may be a shock to some of her friends and to herself. Sometimes women get so caught up in all that's going on in their lives they don't even see the changes that are affecting everyone around them.

Emily's PMDD symptoms are very severe, even though she's still only a teenager. Other women experience a definite increase in PMS symptoms in their thirties and forties, when they begin having children and experiencing stress on a more consistent level. For them the changes sometimes creep up and get out of control before they think to get some help.

Ellen Freeman, research professor in the departments of psychiatry, obstetrics, and gynecology at the University of Pennsylvania Medical School, served as a consultant to the DSM-IV PMDD Work Group. She and her colleagues performed a controlled trial monitoring the benefits of SSRIs, specifically Sarafem (Prozac), on the psychological and physical symptoms of women suffering with PMDD. Using the Penn Daily Symptom Report, those who took the antidepressant scored 50 to 65 percent fewer symptoms than they did when they were not taking the drug; there was only a 29 percent decrease in the placebo group. Freeman also found that those on the tricyclic antidepressant desipramine scored no better than the placebo. Since an antidepressant that does not work to change serotonin levels made no difference for women suffering from PMDD symptoms, it adds to the proof that serotonin plays an important role in PMDD and PMS.

placebo: An inert or innocuous substance used specially in controlled experiments testing the efficacy of another substance as a drug.

Another test, reported by the pharmaceutical company Pfizer, studied Zoloft's effectiveness for treating PMDD. One group used the drug on a daily routine, while the other only used it during the luteal phase the two weeks before the onset of menses. The women studied were given from 50 to 150 milligrams a day, according to their response to the drug and their individual tolerance. Daily use of the drug raised the score of the tests significantly more than those of the women on the placebo. The scores of the women who took Zoloft only during the luteal phase also reflected a positive change.

Maryann is an example of a woman who needed help from SSRIs. She worked for a printing company in an average-size town,

In the nineteenth century, women's lives were expected to re-volve around childbearing.

Women in the early 1880s:

- had seven or eight children.
- breast-fed each one for twelve to eighteen months as a way to prevent another pregnancy as long as possible (a form of birth control that is not always effective).
- experienced menopause near the age of forty.
- usually lived no longer than their late forties (often because their bodies were worn out from childbearing).

Until recently, our culture thought that women's primary job was to produce and raise children. Women's ailments were not taken seriously. With the advent of the women's movement in the twentieth century, however, all that began to change. For the first time, scientists began to research the female body. As a result, our culture—and women themselves—have new respect and understanding for the monthly cycle all women experience.

and her three children attended a local high school. She and her husband enjoyed their neighborhood and local church. Her yard was filled with beautiful flowers inside its white picket fence, and she loved her family's friendly small dog. Life seemed good . . . except lately Maryann had noticed she had more bad days than good ones.

While out to lunch with a friend from work, she commented that she only had about one week a month when she felt really good. Her friend laughed in agreement—but Maryann knew her friend did not have as much trouble with PMS symptoms as she did.

Because of a particularly stressful few months at work and the upcoming graduation of her daughter, Maryann felt even more tense. She found herself unable to sleep night after night. When she did sleep, about once a month she would wake up with a scream that startled the whole family. She dreamed again and again that someone entered her bedroom and stood over her bed.

A woman who is experiencing a premenstrual disorder is more apt to lose her temper with her children and other loved ones.

Maryann became more and more anxious. Her binge eating was hard to control, although she normally prided herself on eating five to six small healthy meals daily. Finally, worn out and so tired she could barely function, Maryann consulted her physician. After the charting and usual medical exams, her physician diagnosed her with PMDD and prescribed Zoloft at 25 milligrams a day, only during her luteal phase.

Within one cycle, Maryann noticed a difference. She was better able to handle her teenage children's schedules; she slept much better; and she felt more like herself than she had in years.

Lois felt like a different person once a month. She fought with her husband over who took the garbage out last and whether he put the pan in the wrong cupboard. She went to bed angry, woke up angry, and nothing in life seemed right. Once her husband brought home dinner to surprise her, since it was her night to cook. Instead of thanking him, she began crying: she was sure he was trying to pacify her because he felt she was incompetent to cook a decent dinner.

But Lois knew her children were the ones who suffered most. During the week or two before her period, her two daughters, a five- and seven-year-old, always watched Lois carefully, afraid to say or do the wrong thing. Normally, when she picked them up from day care, the three of them talked about their day or sang songs or planned an evening of family fun. But for a week or two each month, Lois would always find something that made her yell at the girls. They talked too loud, or they didn't answer her questions, or they bickered with each other until she wanted to scream. On those nights, the drive usually ended in an explosion; both Lois and her girls would run into the house, unable to enjoy anything that evening.

When Lois began taking an SSRI during the luteal phase of her cycle, things changed drastically. She and the girls enjoyed their rides home every night, and the family was able to continue planning a game night and movie night each week throughout the month. They enjoyed short outings to a pumpkin farm and petting zoo. Because Lois felt so much better, she had more energy for everything in her life.

Some people think that PMS was invented by women to excuse their need to "vent" occasionally. However, research shows that PMS and PMDD are very real. Depending on the individual, the severity of symptoms ranges from mild to debilitating. Many women who suffer from PMS will experience problems that lead to relationship difficulties, or they may find it hard to be productive and dependable at school and on the job. But some women suffer such major changes during the later part of the menstrual cycle that those who know them are sometimes terrified by these women's behavior.

For instance, Kendra was a freshman in high school when she first experienced a "fit of anger" that surprised even herself. She had been left home with her five younger siblings while her parents went to a party. Kendra was not happy because she had wanted to attend a party at her best friend's house. One of her brothers was fooling around with the TV remote when suddenly there was no picture; none of the children could produce one, even though they tried continuously for about an hour. Kendra could feel herself get angrier and angrier. Finally, she grabbed her brother's arm and began to twist it behind his back. Then she hit him over and over, screaming, "Why can't you leave anything alone?"

The other children watched with their eyes wide. When she was done, Kendra sent them all to their rooms. She sank down on the floor with her legs tucked under her arms and cried. Her parents came home late and did not discover the television problem until the next day. No one mentioned Kendra's fit.

As time went on, Kendra had various "fits of anger" and began to engage in destructive behavior, almost always during the days right before her menstrual period. Once she stole a motorcycle and sped through a huge empty lot; she remembers thinking, All I want to do is drive all this meanness right out of me. Can't I ever feel good about myself? She drank, started using recreational drugs, and was failing most of her classes—even though she had scored high enough on her SATs to gain a scholarship to a good college.

When she got caught drinking on her college campus, Kendra finally had to look at the issues causing her behavior. She was very fortunate to have been assigned a counselor who knew and cared about women's issues. Her counselor asked questions about Kendra's past, about her eating habits, about her menstrual periods, about relationships, and how Kendra felt about herself. It didn't take the counselor long to help Kendra see the influence her menstrual cycle had on her moods and her decision-making process. The counselor worked with the physician at the school, and Kendra began taking a low dose of an antidepressant.

When she first learned about the PMS and the use of antidepressants to help control the symptoms, Kendra told her counselor, "Just give me the pills and I'll be okay. I don't need to talk about all this

Depression, irritability, and even fits of rage are common symptoms of a premenstrual disorder.

Some young women may "self-medicate" their premenstrual symptoms by abusing alcohol. . .

other junk." But her counselor refused to refer Kendra to a doctor for a prescription for the pills without further sessions. The counselor knew that Kendra's issue was one of body, mind, and spirit working together. The counselor believed that if she could help Kendra see the truth, she would find more positive ways to live and interact with others.

Proper diet, exercise, and counseling allowed Kendra to see that being the eldest of six children and having parents who enjoyed partying and drinking had led her to feel used. She often felt the

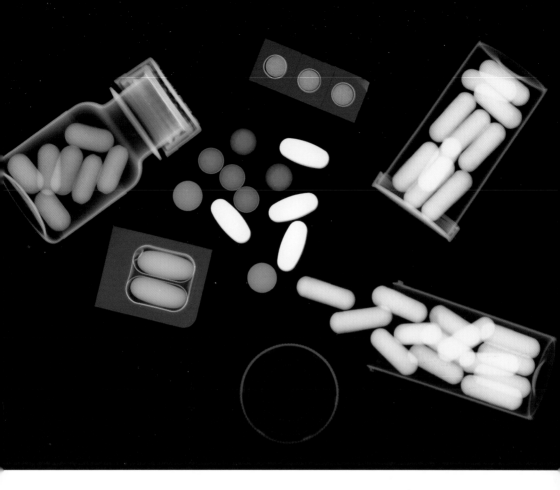

. . . or recreational drugs. Substance abuse will only add to their problems.

younger children were more her responsibility than her parents'. But the counselor didn't stop there; she helped Kendra see that she was responsible for all her decisions and actions, even if she felt terrible because of PMS symptoms or if she were dealing with the irresponsibility of two drunken parents.

As she learned more about her body, Kendra was able to appreciate its complexities. She learned how to use relaxation techniques to help during particularly stressful times. She also learned that her decisions played an important role in how she felt and how she

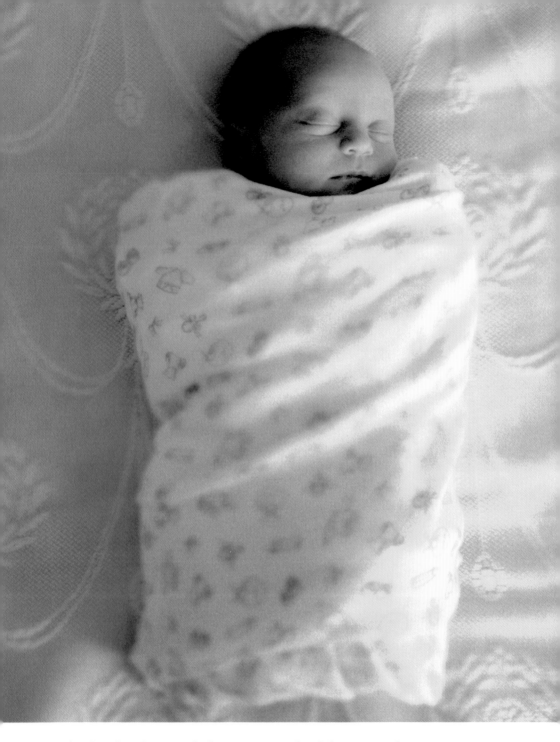

The birth of a new baby is a wonderful event—but it can trigger the onset of PMS symptoms in the baby's mother.

## PMS Symptoms Begin at Different Times for Different Women

Here are some of the life experiences that may coincide with the onset of PMS:

- The first menstrual cycle
- Terminating birth control pills
- Childbirth
- Pregnancy complicated by toxemia (poisonous substance in the blood)
- Miscarriage or abortion
- Trauma (death in the family, chronic disease, accident)
- Perimenopause (nearing menopause but still having a period)

reacted to those things outside herself. She understood at last that she could choose to stay away from bad decisions.

The night she got caught drinking on campus became a turning point for Kendra. She no longer takes an antidepressant but is able to use the lifestyle changes she learned from her counselor to control her PMS anger and deal with the pressures of school, an internship, and her relationships with friends and family.

Women, more than men, tend to feel they are responsible for what goes on around them. As little girls, women are often trained that their job is to make others feel good, to be giving and nurturing so that everyone around them has whatever they need. As a result, women sometimes don't ask for help, because they look at themselves as being the helpers, especially in their role with children.

Psychiatric medication can help women with severe PMS achieve an emotional balance, enabling them to live their lives more productively all month long.

Historically, our culture has also at-
tached a **stigma** to menstruation and
PMS. This meant that for years women
didn't talk about their monthly difficulties. They didn't admit them even
to themselves, and whatever problems they experienced became
sources of guilt and shame.

**stigma**: A mark
of shame or discredit.

Today, however, that is changing. Researchers are taking PMS
very seriously—and they are finding that medication can help
women live their lives more productively all month long. Because
of drugs like Prozac and Zoloft, women like Emily, Lois, and Kendra
have found new hope.

Psychiatric drugs should be used with caution, since side effects are a real possibility. Taking daily medication at the same time each day may diminish the chances of unpleasant side effects.

# Chapter Six

# Risks and Side Effects

Emily Palmer's Journal, April 8

I can't believe this. Just when everything was going so good, I had to get sick. This would have to happen to me. Of course, my doctor says this is okay. We'll give it a week or two, he says, and maybe these stomach pains will go away. It's not terrible but it's not pleasant either. Mom says I shouldn't worry because the doctor knows what's going on and he's probably right, I'll feel better in a week or two.

One week later:

I feel great again. I'm back on the medicine but just like the doctor said, I feel fine. I'm applying tomorrow for a job at the sub shop. I

If a dry mouth is one of the side effects experienced while taking an SSRI, sucking on hard candy, chewing gum, or ice cubes may help.

*hope I get it. I'm tired of baby-sitting and I want to get to see some kids after school (kids my age, not just little kids).*

Not everyone taking the SSRI antidepressants experiences side effects but for some women, mild side effects such as difficulty sleeping, anxiety, weakness, tremors, sweating, nausea, drowsiness, nervousness, or yawning, may be a problem when they first take Prozac or Zoloft. In many cases, these annoyances will go away within a few weeks and may not be serious enough to stop taking the medication. For others, however, the side effects can be severe enough that the discomfort outweighs the effectiveness of the drug.

Mattie is such a person. She began taking one of the SSRI antidepressants in a very low dosage because of her sensitivity to medications of any sort. Her doctor had her start by dividing the pills in half. Each week she increased by a half a tablet until she was taking the 25 milligrams her doctor thought she needed. Once that seemed to be effective but not harmful, Mattie moved in these same low increases until she was at 50 milligrams per day. Her doctor decided she should stay at this level for one month, and they would decide if she needed to change her dose at her next visit.

Both Mattie and her doctor were pleased with the results and neither expected what happened next. About two weeks into that month, Mattie began to develop gas pains each evening. She didn't think much of it until her stools became looser and looser. By the time of her one-month visit, her stools were totally liquid, and she was still experiencing gas pain regularly. Mattie had begun a very bland diet that included foods such as chicken, turkey, rice, bread, applesauce, and bananas, but this wasn't enough to ease her stomach pains. Her physician felt she needed to stop taking the antide-

Anyone who takes psychiatric drugs will have many questions.
Medical practitioners can help answer these as they arise.

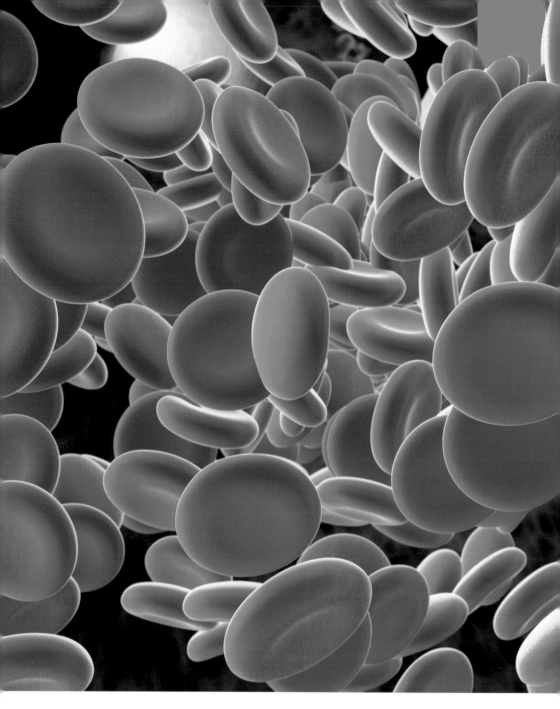

Prozac sometimes decreases the amount of platelets in the blood, making the red blood cells less "sticky." This can cause abnormal bleeding.

> Nothing in our society, with the exception of violence and fear, has been more effective in keeping women in their place than the degradation of the menstrual cycle.
>
> —Christiane Northrup, M.D.

pressant. The constant diarrhea could cause her serious problems (including emotional problems caused by vitamin deficiencies) that might be even worse than her original condition.

Prozac, being the first of the SSRI antidepressants discovered, has received much media attention. Sometimes this leads to misunderstandings about drugs and how they work. Prozac has been so widely prescribed that more than 40 million people in more than 90 countries take this medication to help them live a more effective life. Prozac has undergone many safety and effectiveness studies, so its side effects are well understood. Some people will experience side effects; working closely with a physician is the only way each individual can work out the best treatment for her condition. In Mattie's case, her physician prescribed another of the SRRIs and that worked fine at a low-level dose.

Although it is not known why, SSRIs affect blood platelets, which are important in the **coagulation** of blood. Because of this effect, some patients have experienced abnormal bleeding while using the drug. Although not a typical symptom, any bleeding should be mentioned immediately to the physician.

> **coagulation:** The clotting capability of the blood.

Because SSRIs are broken down in the liver, patients with liver disease must use caution when taking the drug, using lower dosages at the start of the drug therapy.

Some antidepressants can cause serious side effects when combined with other medications. Care must be taken when using these medications with any other drugs, including over-the-counter or natural medications. These include the natural antidepressants such as SAM-e and Saint-John's-wort. In this case, more is not better but may lead to problems worse than PMS symptoms. Alcohol should be avoided or used cautiously when taking antidepressants.

Because antidepressants are not sedatives (that is, they do not cause drowsiness or foggy thinking), driving or performing other hazardous jobs should not be a problem while taking these medications. Nevertheless, caution should be used until the correct dosage has been determined to be sure of the effects of any drug. As has been mentioned before, medication affects each person differently.

Women who might become pregnant should be aware that few

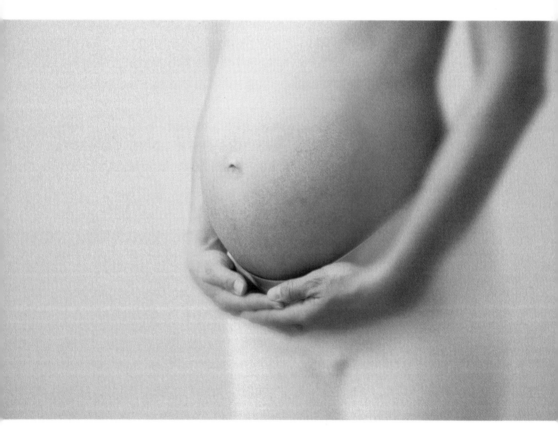

A woman and her doctor should carefully assess her need for psychiatric drugs during pregnancy.

If a nursing mother is taking an SSRI, the drug will pass through her milk to the baby.

studies have been done on the effects of SSRIs on developing fetuses. Some researchers are currently studying antidepressant use during pregnancy, but no conclusions have been reached. The risks must be discussed with the physician. However, some studies have been done on the effect of SSRIs on breastfeeding, and the drug was found to pass to a baby through breast milk.

One problem that is often overlooked in treatment with antidepressants is withdrawal symptoms. Just as most people should gradually increase their dose when they are beginning an antidepressant, they should also gradually decrease their dose when they are going off it. A discontinuation syndrome is associated with terminating the use of antidepressants. Some of the symptoms include dizziness, stomach problems, sleep disturbances, nightmares, anxiety, irritability, numbness, or other unusual sensations. Because the symptoms can be signs of other diseases as well, misdiagnosis is

Whenever a woman takes a psychiatric drug for PMS symptoms, she should be careful to discuss with her medical practitioner any side effects she experiences.

common.

As with anything that alters body functions, antidepressants must be monitored by a physician. Finding the right doctor and keeping her aware of any changes experienced while taking an SSRI is the best way to eliminate concern over side effects. A slow start up and a slow discontinuation both help protect patients from unnecessary problems. Like Emily's physician did, any good doctor will help make necessary changes to improve treatment. This may involve switching from medication to medication or from one dose to another.

Thanks to appropriate treatment for their PMS symptoms, young women like Emily Palmer can resume normal social lives.

# Chapter Seven

# Alternative Treatments for PMS

E mily Palmer's Journal, May 3

*Well, I really feel like myself again. I can't believe that for so long I couldn't see what was happening to me. I was so mean sometimes, but I guess because I couldn't understand what was going on, I just made excuses for myself. Anyway, things are so much better. Sarah and I are really close now. About a month ago she asked me to start power walking every afternoon after school. She told me she read that walking was helpful for women who suffered from PMS. She figured we might as well give it a try 'cause she'd been feeling like a wimp from not doing any regular exercise herself. We both love it and we hardly ever miss a day.*

*I'm even dating Mark. I guess he decided even though I was such a jerk at Homecoming, I have some redeeming character.*

*Anyway, all month long now I feel almost the same. I still know when it is getting close to the time for my period, but I'm not mean, I can concentrate on my schoolwork just as well as any other time of the month, and best of all I feel like myself, not some PMS monster.*

*I guess I've learned to like doctors better, too. It's amazing to me that they know so much about so many different things, like how the brain works and how food and exercise can make a difference for just one problem. What about all the other things people suffer from? I wonder if I ought to become a doctor. I've always just thought of sick people as mostly having colds and flu and strep throat, but the way my doctor brought this all together for me has been so cool. I think I'd like to help others that way too.*

Taking a medication like Zoloft for two weeks out of her cycle really helped Emily make the necessary changes in her lifestyle. But her doctor realized she needed to do some physical work herself and advised her to follow some new dietary practices and to get regular exercise. Food choices and exercise do so much to help a person feel healthier that almost everyone can feel better by adhering to a few recommendations from those who have studied the effects of diet and exercise on the body.

# Treating PMS with Food

For those who want to try an alternative that is relatively easy to follow and does not cause major risks or side effects, food is a good choice. Anyone can obtain information from a physician, a dietician, and from well-researched books applauding the benefits of a good diet. (Diet, in this case, refers to the usual food and drink a person consumes each day to stay alive.) In some cases, a woman may try to lose weight or may simply notice a loss of weight because of better food, more healthy choices. Losing weight is not the immediate

Being comfortable with yourself requires more than simply taking a pill. Diet, exercise, and other forms of treatment all play a role in a healthy lifestyle.

goal, though; instead, eating food in combinations that influence the body's chemistry, help balance hormones, and feed the nervous system is the objective. The best food choices to accomplish this goal include those that are fresh, unrefined, and unprocessed.

In her book *The Serotonin Solution*, Dr. Judith Wurtman, from the Massachusetts Institute of Technology, shares information from more than fifteen years of research on the effects of carbohydrates on emotions, the appetite, and mood. Much of her work has centered on weight-loss programs. Through these studies, she found that the changes in the brain, mainly in the serotonin level, regulate mood, appetite, and even the self-control one has over eating

Women who are experiencing premenstrual symptoms often crave carbohydrates. Eating a piece of bread will often ease their feelings of depression.

Dairy products are a good source of protein. Combined with a healthy diet of carbohydrates, they may help decrease premenstrual food cravings.

Spaghetti and other pasta are a good source of carbohydrates.

choices and bingeing. Because so many PMS sufferers craved carbohydrates during the last part of their luteal phase, Dr. Wurtman studied nineteen PMS sufferers who lived with her at her labs for forty-eight hours before and after the onset of their periods. She measured their food intake and monitored the types of food each woman ate.

Dr. Wurtman found that before their periods the women chose carbohydrates more often than they did after their periods began. She also tested the effect of carbohydrates on mood by giving premenstrual women a bowl of cornflakes with nondairy creamer. The women who were melancholy and tired became more alert and happier.

With this knowledge and the studies she had already performed, Dr. Wurtman began to study the influence of food on serotonin lev-

If a woman experiences feelings of sadness or despair during the week before she menstruates, regular small snacks can help her maintain a better emotional balance.

Strenuous exercise affects brain chemistry.

els. She found that by eating the right combination of foods—lots of carbohydrates with moderate proteins—at certain times throughout the day, the volunteers gained a sense of well-being and reduced food cravings.

Before her death in 2004, Dr. Katharina Dalton was another advocate for controlling PMS symptoms with diet. As was mentioned earlier, Dr. Dalton was one of the forerunners in studying PMS and for many years played a significant role in its treatment. Dalton believed in the 3-Hourly Starch Diet. She said that women should never go longer than five hours between eating, while women suffering with PMS symptoms need to eat more frequently, having small meals or snacks that must include starches. For those who worry about consuming extra calories, she suggested eating only half a sandwich at lunch and saving the other half for a mid-afternoon snack. This eating regimen regulates blood sugar levels, keeping them even rather than too high or too low. Dr. Dalton encouraged her patients to carry emergency supplies of food with them at all times. Then if a woman is caught in traffic, held up at a meeting, or just running late doing errands, she has food with her to maintain her blood sugar level. She also insisted that women keep to this diet routine throughout their menstrual cycle. She insisted it would not work unless adhered to on a regular basis. Besides the benefits to PMS symptoms, eating small meals has been proven to lower cholesterol and increase weight loss.

In another book, called *Natural Prozac*, author Dr. Joel Robertson shares information from studies that show various foods, activities, thoughts, and behaviors can influence the brain's chemistry. Athletes experience a high from strenuous activity; persons who experience a traumatic event experience emotional backlash for days or weeks afterward, and when you have a fight with a friend you may feel upset for an hour or even days afterward. All of these may alter

## Other Alternative Treatments

Those who treat the body using homeopathy create the symptoms that match those of the patient in order to allow the body to heal itself. So rather than treat the symptoms, a homeopath hopes to create an environment where the body uses its own healing powers. This treatment has been used for PMS with some success.

An acupuncturist works with a form of Chinese medicine in which needles are inserted into the body at certain points to help bring balance to the body's energy flow. Acupuncture has also been used to treat the symptoms of PMS.

An acupuncturist inserts needles to restore the body's normal energy flow.

Something as simple as a bowl of cereal can help ease the ill temper of a woman suffering from menstrual disorders.

the brain's chemistry—and again, specific chemicals may be involved, which is why antidepressants are used to treat some disorders where the brain chemical activity is not working properly. But some physicians and researchers believe these brain chemicals can be altered without medication.

One of the quickest ways to change transmitters such as serotonin naturally

dopamine: A monoamine, $C_8H_{11}NO_2$, that is a decarboxylated form of dopa and that occurs especially as a neurotransmitter in the brain.

is with food choices. Some scientists believe that altering just one meal can make a difference. Eating foods rich in protein elevates the dopamine and norepinephrine levels in the brain. Protein is converted into amino acids, which are the building blocks for the brain's transmitters. This change can take place in just minutes. Red meats contain large amounts of tryptophan, the necessary amino acid for the brain's transmitters, but they also contain other amino acids that compete to get into the brain. Without the addition of carbohydrates to enhance the absorption of the amino acid tryptophan, there is no benefit. That's why eating carbohydrates along with proteins is important.

Even though a carbohydrate like a chocolate cookie or a doughnut may immediately medicate moods, whole grains such as brown rice, oats, barley, and whole-wheat bread and noodles are the best foods to eat. The body quickly absorbs foods made with processed sugars and flours, rapidly elevating blood sugar levels. Then, blood sugar levels quickly drop again. The body takes longer to digest and absorb whole-grain foods, and so the nervous system reaps the benefits of good feelings, greater concentration, and often increased relaxation over a greater time period.

Sandra had been experiencing PMS symptoms for years. Most of the time she felt under control, although later, when they were older, her children told her they had learned to stay clear of Mom during "those times of the month." Happy that they understood the problem, Sandra's guilt level lessened over the years. But she suffered from feeling ill for about two weeks of the month. After much reading and research, Sandra decided to try a diet of complex carbohydrates, eliminating as much refined sugar as she could from her diet. She stopped drinking beverages with caffeine and—most difficult of all—she drastically cut back her chocolate intake.

After a few weeks of successes and bingeing failures, Sandra finally got control of her eating. Not long after, she noticed she felt better than she had in a long time. She also noticed that her clothes

When a woman achieves emotional balance all month long, her
family will notice the difference.

Exercise increases energy levels, reduces stress, and improves metabolism.

fit great and she did not feel so tired in the late afternoon. About two months after she began her food changes, her daughter said to her, "Mom, this new you is great. You're like yourself most of the time. I don't have to run upstairs when you walk in the door any more."

# Lifestyles Make a Difference

Different social, personal, and business activities also affect neurotransmitters. When a person goes to an amusement park, most generally the activity makes one excited enough to increase norepinephrine and dopamine levels. The same happens at a dance, where it is difficult to fight the impulse to move. Fast-moving exercise and entertainment can lift one's mood. In order to make a difference in serotonin levels, however, the activity needs to be more sedate and calming, like listening to soft music. When the activities provide a relaxed atmosphere, serotonin levels elevate.

Exercise can be an extremely successful option in the treatment of PMS. Exercise quickly changes the energy levels of those involved. Many women use the excuse that they can't exercise because they are too tired—and yet exercise may be the catalyst to an energy increase that will eventually lead to increased productivity. Suddenly, it may be easier to get schoolwork done. Women feel they have more energy for their families and friends, as well as the duties of a home and school or work. The increased productivity improves self-esteem, which creates a positive cycle of growth.

Exercise may also reduce binge eating by reducing stress levels and increasing the endorphins that help create a more positive and self-assured attitude. Exercise enables the body to better metabolize whatever sugars are consumed. And of course a good workout— whether it is a brisk walk, aerobics, or jogging—helps with weight control. Again, this may not be the most important goal, but less body fat improves general health.

Dr. Michelle Harrison, an assistant professor of psychiatry at the University of Pittsburgh School of Medicine and author of Self-Help for Premenstrual Syndrome, did not originally believe that diet could play a significant role in helping women suffering with PMS. But when she saw a similarity between the symptoms of PMS and low blood sugar (hypoglycemia), Dr. Harrison created a high-carbohydrate diet of whole grains, fruits, vegetables, potatoes, and pasta that also eliminated sugar, caffeine, alcohol, and artificial sweeteners. The effect this diet had on her patients was encouraging, giving long sought-after relief.

# Psychological Therapy

This is an often overlooked treatment for PMS and PMDD. Sometimes an underlying problem is magnified when a premenstrual woman begins to feel more agitated and more physically stressed. One woman describes the feeling this way: "It's as though there was a radio always playing at the back of my mind. It's always there, all that stuff that gets me so upset, but most of the time I can ignore it. When I'm premenstrual, though, it's like the volume's turned up so loud that it's the only thing I can hear." Getting psychological help for the underlying problem may help a woman be in better control of her PMS symptoms.

Counselors offer this type of help. There are many different types—psychologists, social workers, and priests, ministers, and even laypeople within the church are often trained to help one see the truth about situations. They can also help to open up lines of communication within families. Counselors with an undergraduate degree in social work have the initials B.S.W.; if they've attained a master's degree in social work, the letters M.S.W. follow their name. These counselors have worked under observed settings learning the skills needed to help others. Counselors who have their doctorate have spent a longer time in training and have a medical background, but they are not physicians and cannot prescribe medications. Psychiatrists are both counselors and medical doctors. They have studied mental disorders but have also had four years of medical training. They can prescribe medications as well as provide counsel.

Each of these persons may be able to provide extra help in managing stress levels and uncovering misconceptions from childhood or adulthood. Counselors can also help a woman to see where she fits into her family, work, and social settings by giving her the skills to see the truth of her value as an individual, whatever her position.

Stress-management classes teach participants how to channel the tension, stress, and anger of PMS. Breathing exercises and relaxation techniques work to not only calm the woman immediately but also to teach the body what a state of relaxation feels like, helping to reprogram it during times of extreme tension.

# Hormones

Treatment that includes the hormone progesterone has made a significant change in the PMS symptoms for some women. Dr. Dalton advocates the use of progesterone along with her 3-Hourly Starch Diet for those women who need more than just diet and exercise. Because of the absence of severe side effects, women can try natural progesterone without fear.

Some physicians prescribe oral contraceptives (birth control pills) to help alleviate PMS symptoms. Because they work for some women and not others, they must be used on a trial basis. If they don't work, another treatment might. Some women become depressed while taking birth control pills, or a woman may have a health condition that makes birth control pills an additional risk factor, so birth control pills are not the best choice for everyone.

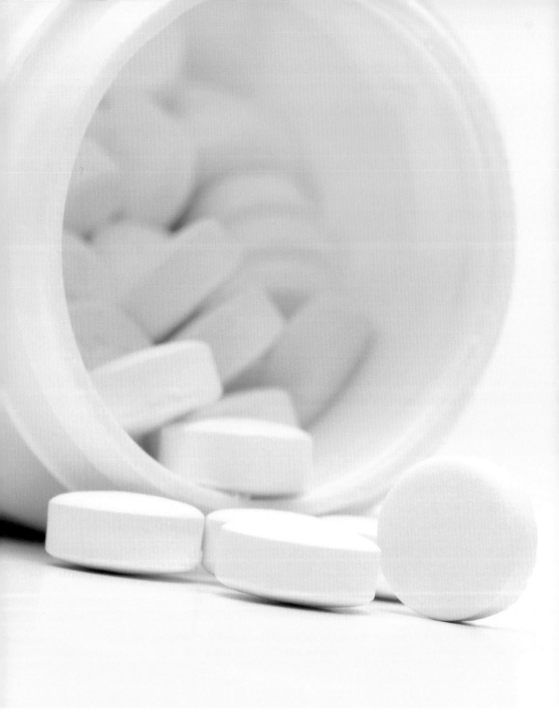

Anti-inflammatory drugs like aspirin and ibuprofen can help ease premenstrual symptoms.

# Medications Other Than Antidepressants

Anti-inflammatory drugs include ibuprofen and aspirin, which can be purchased over-the-counter or given in higher doses that require a prescription. Other prescription anti-inflammatory drugs are also available. Used for pain and inflammation, the drugs work better if begun the day before symptoms appear.

If a woman tries several different types of these drugs and finds no relief, she must assume they are not the right choice for her particular symptoms. Although many women do find relief using them, not everyone does.

For stomach bloating, diuretics prove very useful. Diuretics reduce swelling and water retention and have even reduced depression somewhat in certain women.

On some occasions physicians prescribe anti-anxiety medications to help with insomnia, irritability, and tension. Although they must be used with supervision because of their addictive nature, they help women who don't seem to be helped by other treatments. One reason they may produce significant overall changes in PMS patients is the fact that sleep plays such an important role in dealing with any health problems. Anti-anxiety drugs are sedatives. Proper rest precedes good health.

# Vitamins and Minerals

Nutritional supplements have become a large part of many Americans' overall health care. Several studies have investigated which supplements work best to help PMS. Vitamin B6 has been one of the most controversial. Some women insist the vitamin reduces symptoms, but only about half of the studies indicate any verifiable relief from this vitamin. Care must be taken with the dosage of this vitamin to avoid harmful side effects.

## Foods to Avoid When Suffering from PMS:

- caffeine (coffees, teas, colas, and chocolate)
- refined sugar
- smoked and processed meats
- deep-fried foods
- foods high in sodium (salt)

## Foods to Enjoy When Suffering from PMS:

- whole grains
- fresh fruits
- fresh vegetables
- pasta
- potatoes
- nuts, seeds
- protein (lean meat, eggs, cheese)
- fish
- plenty of water

Many North American women have a deficiency of magnesium. Magnesium supplementation may help PMS headaches as well as decrease chocolate cravings. The best way to get any nutrients—whether vitamins or minerals—is through the food consumed each day.

## Natural Treatments

Many natural substances have been used for centuries to treat premenstrual symptoms. Evening primrose oil is one example that has

Saint-John's-wort is a natural remedy for depression.

been used by many women to help PMS. Called the natural anti-depressant, there is much controversy over its effectiveness. Saint-John's-wort is another "natural" antidepressant.

The herb vitex is believed to help regulate the menstrual cycle by increasing the levels of estrogen and progesterone. (It also helps when menstrual bleeding is a problem, and shrinks fibroid tumors in some women.) Another substance used to stimulate the secretion of estrogen and progesterone is black cohosh root. It is also thought to help with water retention, improve digestion, and calm women—but it has the side effect of causing a heavy menstrual flow.

As with any of the natural and herb remedies, these substances must be used with caution. Just because something is said to be natural does not mean it is better. When more aggressive treatment is needed, women should consult someone they can trust before beginning any vitamin or herbal remedy.

# Light Therapy

Studies have been done on the relationship between seasonal affective disorder (SAD) and PMS. Many of the symptoms are very similar: those who suffer from SAD crave sugary and starchy foods; they are depressed, sad, and sometimes irritable. Both their sleeping and eating habits are affected, and their symptoms exist only at certain times (in this case when the days are shorter and there is less light). During the spring and summer these symptoms disappear.

While researching different methods for treating PMS, one study used a bright-light procedure much like that used on SAD patients. The women responded well and noticed differences in weight gain, depression, carbohydrate cravings, fatigue, and irritability. Another study that used two hours of bright light daily in the morning showed improvement in PMS symptoms. Others noticed that natural light made a difference—especially for those who spend much of their time under artificial lights either at work, school, or recreation.

Emily's story has a happy ending. She was able to move beyond her symptoms to feel better and to learn how to deal with others in personal relationships.

Thanks to the scientists who have researched the way the brain works, women no longer have to simply suffer through their PMS symptoms each month. Today many different treatments exist; physicians, counselors, and support groups offer both help and encouragement. Women can learn to understand their monthly changes, achieving not only acceptance but also empowerment and self-control.

# Further Reading

Berkow, Robert, Beers, Mark, and Andrew J. Fletcher, eds. *The Merck Manual of Medical Information—Home Edition*. New York: Simon & Schuster, 2004.

Dalton, Katharina. *Once a Month*. Alameda, Calif.: Hunter House, 1999.

Griffith, H. Winter. *Complete Guide to Prescription & Nonprescription Drugs 2012*. New York: Penguin, 2011.

Kramer, Peter D. *Listening to Prozac.* New York: Penguin, 1997.

*Professional Guide to Disease*. Ambler, Penn.: Lippincott Williams & Wilkins, 2013.

Pintus, Lorraine. *Jump Off the Hormone Swing*. Chicago: Moody Publications, 2011.

Rybacki, James J. *The Essential Guide to Prescription Drugs 2002*. New York: HarperCollins, 2000.

Semler, Tracy Chutorian. *All About Eve: The Complete Guide to Women's Health and Well-Being*. Nashville, Tenn.: Thomas Nelson Publishing, 2001.

Taylor, Diana and Stacey Colino. *Taking Back the Month: A Personalized Solution for Managing PMS and Enhancing Your Health*. New York: The Berkeley Publishing Group, 2002.

# For More Information

Canadian Mental Health Association, Nova Scotia Division
www.cmhans.org

Methodist Health Care System (Gynecology)
www.methodisthealth.com/whs.cfm?id=35898

Museum of Menstruation and Women's Health
www.mum.org/index.html

Psychology Information Online
www.psychologyinfo.com/depression/index.html

Womenshealth.gov (PMS)
womenshealth.gov/publications/our-publications/fact-sheet/
premenstrual-syndrome.cfm

Publisher's Note:
The websites listed on this page were active at the time of publication. The publisher is not responsible for websites that have changed their address or discontinued operation since the date of publication. The publisher will review and update the websites upon each reprint.

# Index

# About the Author & Consultants

Sherry Bonnice lives with her husband and two children on a dirt road in rural Pennsylvania. They raise rabbits and have a small farm with a goat, a sheep, chickens, one duck, five dogs, and two cats. Sherry has co-edited quilt magazines and written a quilt book. She has also written several books for other Mason Crest series, including Careers with Character and North American Folklore.

Mary Ann McDonnell, Ph.D., R.N., is the owner of South Shore Psychiatric Services, where she provides psychiatric services to children and adolescents. She has worked as a psychiatric nurse at Franciscan Hospital for Children and has been a clinical instructor for Northeastern University and Boston College advanced-practice nursing students. She was also the director of clinical trials in the pediatric psychopharmacology research unit at Massachusetts General Hospital. Her areas of expertise are bipolar disorder in children and adolescents, ADHD, and depression.

Donald Esherick has worked in regulatory affairs at Rhone-Poulenc Rorer, Wyeth Pharmaceuticals, Pfizer, and Pharmalink Consulting. He specializes in the chemistry section (manufacture and testing) of investigational and marketed drugs.